The Placemakers of Hong Kong

The Placemakers of Hong Kong

Roger Nissim

Commentaries by Nelson Chen

Hong Kong University Press
The University of Hong Kong
Pok Fu Lam Road
Hong Kong
https://hkupress.hku.hk

© 2025 Hong Kong University Press

ISBN 978-988-8876-86-0 (*Paperback*)

All rights reserved. No portion of this publication may be reproduced or transmitted in any form or by any means, electronic or mechanical, including photocopying, recording, or any information storage or retrieval system, without prior permission in writing from the publisher.

Every effort has been made to identify and contact copyright holders to obtain permission for the use of copyrighted material. The authors apologize for any errors or omissions in this process and welcome notifications of corrections or required permissions, which will be incorporated into future reprints or editions of this book.

British Library Cataloguing-in-Publication Data
A catalogue record for this book is available from the British Library.

Digitally printed

Contents

Foreword by Sr Chiu Kam Kuen	vi
The Placemakers of Hong Kong: Introduction, Background, and Definition for Hong Kong	viii
1. Hongkong Land's Footbridge Network in Central	1
2. Swire Properties: Taikoo Place	15
3. Twin Towers: Gateway Entry into Victoria Harbour	28
4. Lai Chi Wo: Exemplar of Sustainable Cultural Heritage Conservation	42
5. Transformation of the New Territories and Development of the Nine New Towns	62
6. The Future: Northern Metropolis Development Strategy	83
Afterword: From Space to Place and Humane Urbanism	104

Foreword

The Hong Kong Institute of Surveyors is both pleased and proud to be involved with the publication of this book under its book-writing sponsorship initiative, because it considers it to be a suitable textbook relevant to local practice for the surveying industry and students.

The author, Sr Roger Nissim FHKIS, FRICS, was, in fact, a founding member of the Institute back in 1984. He brings his fifty years' worth of broad local real estate experience to the research and writing of this book, having worked in both the public and private sectors, and in the latter years, academia. In fact, the recent years have been very productive for him, as *The First Estates: The Story of Fairview Park and Hong Lok Yuen with Documents* was published in 2020; this book was followed by the fifth edition of his well-known *Land Administration and Practice in Hong Kong* in 2022. Both volumes were also published by Hong Kong University Press.

This book will serve a number of different purposes; firstly, as a reminder and statement of what local development companies, charitable organizations, as well as the government have been able to achieve in contributing to the enhancement of Hong Kong's evolving urban and rural landscape over the last few decades. Secondly, the book will be a useful teaching tool as it showcases five completed, contrasting case studies. The final case study examines the government's imaginative and creative plans for the future Northern Metropolis. It has potential, if executed properly, to be a very significant example of placemaking on a huge scale over the coming two decades. Thus, the book should provide suitable reference material for both students and practitioners not only in the surveying field but also those in the architectural, urban design, and planning fields.

Finally, with its good range of visuals, the book will also be of interest to the wider Hong Kong public who may wish to better understand the story behind each of the six case studies presented.

Sr CHIU Kam Kuen
President (2021–2022)
Hong Kong Institute of Surveyors

The Placemakers of Hong Kong: Introduction, Background, and Definition for Hong Kong

Introduction

Since the inception and adoption of the term 'placemaking' by urban planners, architects, and landscape architects in the early 1970s, its primary use evolved as a community design and community development tool with special focus on urban public spaces.

The history of placemaking in the urban cities of the USA can, in fact, be traced back to the ground-breaking work in the 1960s of urban activists like Jane Jacobs (1916–2016) and William H Whyte (1917–1999). Jacob's best-known and most influential work, *The Death and Life of Great American Cities*, was first published in 1961 as a critique of 1950s urban planning policy. Together, they started to introduce the idea of designing cities for people, not just for cars and shopping centres. Their work focused on the social and cultural importance of lively neighbourhoods and inviting public spaces: Jacobs encouraged everyday citizens to take ownership of the streets through her now famous idea of 'eyes on the streets', which was that in order for a street to be a safe place, 'there must be eyes upon the street, eyes belonging to those who we might call the natural proprietors of the street' (Jacobs 1961, 3).

Jacobs' common-sense approach argued in favour of high-density mixed developments, saying that the mixture of workplaces and residences within a single neighbourhood generally assures the public that there are always people around keeping streets safe with their presence. She also states that there should be stores, bars, cafes, and restaurants within the same neighbourhoods and that 'cities have a capability of providing something for everybody, only because, and only when, they are created by everybody' (Jacobs 1961, 238).

In a recent biography of William H Whyte entitled *American Urbanist,* Richard K Rein notes that Whyte's keen eye for urban observation and clear, insightful writing on human behaviour in public spaces both preceded and enabled Jacobs to write as she did, as his key elements for creating vibrant social life in public spaces, such as bottom-up place design, aligned with hers. He was also an instrumental figure in getting her book published in 1961. Whyte was considered to be the mentor at the establishment of the Project for Public Places, whose work is discussed below.

Building on the wisdom of these two urban pioneers and others, a more collaborative community process emerged for creating and revitalizing public spaces. The process is centred around observing, listening to, and asking questions of the people who live, work, and play in a particular space in order to better understand their needs and aspirations for that space and for their community as a whole. With this knowledge, it is possible to create a common vision for that place.

However, it must be remembered that the Hong Kong situation is probably unique, with the Hong Kong Special Administrative Region Government being such a dominant player in the overall development of the territory (as Chapters 5 and 6 demonstrate), as well as being the landlord of all private land under the leasehold land system. All of this has resulted in rather rigid planning processes evolving over the past thirty-plus years that have become so institutionalized that community stakeholders and grassroot representatives have rarely had a meaningful chance to voice their own ideas and aspirations about the place they inhabit. The public planning consultation exercises that have been done locally in recent years are often seen as being purely cosmetic, with the government officials being very reluctant to take on board any criticisms or suggestions for change. This is regrettable because, done properly, such consultation and placemaking exercises would help break down the separate silos of city planners, architects, landscape architects, traffic engineers, building experts, land administrators, and urban designers, encouraging them to look beyond the narrow focus of their own professions, disciplines, and agendas with the objective of designing schemes for the benefit of the community as a whole. It is in this context that Hong Kong has had to develop its own version of placemaking, remembering that here real estate is more expensive than almost any other place in the world and therefore that public spaces come at a premium.

The American experiences reveal that common problems such as traffic-dominated streets, little-used parks, and isolated or underperforming development projects can be addressed, or altogether avoided, by embracing a model of placemaking that views a place in its entirety rather than zeroing in on isolated components.

Based on forty years of practical experience, the Project for Public Spaces (pps.org) has developed a number of principles of placemaking that offer guidelines to help communities. They can be summarized as follows: integrate diverse opinions into a cohesive vision; translate that vision into a plan and program of uses; and ensure a sustainable implementation of the plan. Turning a shared vision into reality – into a truly great place – means finding the patience to take small steps, to seriously listen, and to see what works best in a particular context.

Differentiating rural placemaking from the urban, the Project for Public Spaces gives the following thoughts and guidelines: 'Rural placemaking efforts must also focus on creating new, quality places by engaging all members of the community . . . the process – of consultation, mobilization and engagement – are just as important as the final outcome'.

Again, in the Hong Kong context, both the pre- and post-handover governments have operated very much on the principle that 'big brother knows best', so that the scope for meaningful community participation in the planning process has been very limited. Fortunately, the example of rural placemaking in Chapter 4 of this book demonstrates clearly how the non-governmental organisations (NGOs) involved have been able to more closely follow the original principles set out in the opening paragraphs.

In the end, the simplest contemporary definition of placemaking that I have found, courtesy of Mark A Wyckoff, former professor at Michigan State University Land Policy Institute, seems to be the most appropriate one to adopt for both the urban and rural Hong Kong examples: 'Placemaking is the process of creating quality places where people want to live, work, play, shop, learn and visit' (Wyckoff 2014).

Today, it is recognized that all place-based projects should rightly be considered as a form of placemaking if they are carefully designed with a physical form, are appropriate for their location, and have the potential to improve the local quality of life and attractiveness for additional development and redevelopment. Such placemaking thus has considerable utility as an economic development tool that both enables and encourages private sector participation as demonstrated by the three examples contained in this book: Hongkong Land's Central Footbridges, which came first and set the standard for such networks, followed by the Swire Group's redevelopment at Taikoo Place, and then Sun Hung Kai Properties' Twin Towers.

A feature of contemporary private sector developments in Hong Kong is the design of podium style buildings, which can have the effect of isolating them from neighbouring developments. The three private sector developments studied in this book show how the developers have attempted to overcome this problem by creating a network of pedestrian bridge links between adjoining properties that they also own in order to connect a series of buildings in an attractive way. This results in a positive act of placemaking that benefits all parties concerned: the tenants, the owners, and the passing public.

A word on how these examples were selected and chosen – the three private sector chapters were all case studies that I got to understand as I used and visited them regularly during my adjunct professorship for the Development Projects module of the MSc (Real Estate) course at the University of Hong Kong (2007–2017). As District Lands Officer in Sha Tin from 1980–1984 I was very closely involved with the development of that particular New Town and was naturally aware of the whole New Town development program in progress at that time. More recently, I have been a member of the Board of The Hong Kong Countryside Foundation since its inception in 2011 and have been privileged to see first-hand the Lai Chi

Wo project start and grow and continue to grow into, arguably, our leading example of rural placemaking.

It is worth pointing out that some of the older examples included in the book, such as the Central Footbridges, the Twin Towers, and the Nine New Towns, were designed and built before the concepts of placemaking and placekeeping were fully accepted and adopted in Hong Kong. However, a retrospective analysis has been able to show how they can, in fact, now be described in these contemporary terms. A good example can be found in Chapter 3, 'The Evolution of ICC's Master Planning'.

The final chapter of the book describes the planning of the Northern Metropolis Development Strategy (NMDS), which sets out the government's ambitious, large-scale vision for the future development that aims to more closely connect Hong Kong with neighbouring Shenzhen so that, together, they can become the innovation and technology hub for the Greater Bay Area.

In 2016, Mark Wyckoff co-authored and published *Placemaking as an Economic Development Tool: A Placemaking Guidebook,* which supports the idea that placemaking should now be seen as a key component for predominantly economic development purposes; that means population, jobs, and income growth, with special focus on talent attraction and retention (Wyckoff 2016).

The NMDS would seem to fit in well with this contemporary form of strategic placemaking, hence its inclusion in the book.

Placekeeping

In helping prepare the chapter on Taikoo Place, Swire Properties Ltd (Swire Properties), quite correctly, emphasized the importance to them of not only creating the original physical form of placemaking but also the need to give equal emphasis and resources to managing, maintaining, and constantly updating and improving the spaces they have created with a vigorous regime of placekeeping.

Placekeeping itself is a relatively new concept. Its theories can be traced back to Mel Burton and Nicola Dempsey, who published a paper entitled 'Defining Placemaking: The Long-Term Management of Public Spaces' in *Urban Forestry and Urban Greening* (2012). From their abstract:

> There has long been a focus in urban landscape and design on the creation of high-quality public space, or placemaking. Large amounts of capital continue to be spent on creating such spaces without adequate thought or resources for their long-term maintenance and management of public spaces, or placekeeping. While there may be continued policy rhetoric about the importance of placekeeping, particularly as public spaces are recognized for their important contribution to health, wellbeing, biodiversity and also their economic value, this has not however been supported in practice. There are examples in many cities where

public spaces are subject to poor management and maintenance practices. This is clearly visible where vandalism, litter, and damage to facilities and equipment occur, and people no longer feel safe or comfortable. Placekeeping is not simply about the physical environment, its design and maintenance, but also encompasses the interrelated and non-physical dimensions of partnerships, governance, funding, policy and evaluation. (Burton and Dempsey 2012, 11)

In 2016–17, the US Department of Arts and Culture gave their definition of placekeeping as 'the active care and maintenance of a place and its social fabric by the people who live and work there. It is not just preserving buildings but keeping cultural memories associated with a locale alive, while supporting the ability of the local people to maintain their way of life as they choose.' (U.S. Department of Arts and Culture 2016).

The Lai Chi Wo project described in Chapter 4 of this book helps demonstrate an excellent Hong Kong example of this.

The six very different projects being included in this book help showcase these concepts, and, at the same time, help reinforce Hong Kong's unique identity. In this regard, I am deeply indebted to Professor Nelson Chen FAIA FRIBA FHKIA, former director of the School of Architecture at the Chinese University of Hong Kong (whose commentaries hereafter are annotated 'NC'), in his role as my academic commentator, for his thoughtful critique of each of the chapters where he compares and contrasts each of the projects against international examples and practice, and for the apposite historical perspectives he gives.

In addition, he has kindly written an Afterword to help enhance our understanding of how Hong Kong has evolved in the past and may continue to evolve in the coming decades – all of which adds to the academic rigour of the book and will be well appreciated by fellow academics, students, practitioners, as well as general readers.

I am both grateful and appreciative of the cooperation I have received from Hongkong Land, Swire Properties, and Sun Hung Kai Properties with the provision of critical historical data as well as some of the visual images. This collaboration has helped ensure the accuracy of the text.

It is important to acknowledge the vital contribution that good quality private sector developments have done with regard to placemaking and placekeeping. It has to be accepted that these developers are not totally altruistic and are, ultimately, driven by profit. But as demonstrated with these three companies, they can also have a purpose beyond profit, such as now fully embracing the concepts of sustainable development with strong commitments to Environmental, Social, and Corporate Governance (ESG). Hong Kong has gone through a very difficult period in recent years dealing with, and then slowly recovering from, the ongoing impacts of the COVID-19 pandemic. A review of the annual reports of the three private companies referred to above, covering the period up until the end of 2022, reveals that they were all able to describe the performance of their respective investment portfolios as being 'resilient' to these impacts. The quality of their respective placemaking and placekeeping has thus proven to make good business sense, so the two objectives are not mutually exclusive but are, in fact, a classic win-win scenario.

In support of the above points, reference should also be made to recent comments made by the Urban Land Institute Hong Kong (hongkong@uli.org), who form part of an international membership-based, non-profit making research and educational organization, and who, in their Submission to the Chief Executive Elect in April 2022, observed that: 'For many decades, the private sector has played a major role in the building of the new towns and related infrastructure. For example, the tremendously successful delivery of Sha Tin New Town and Tseung Kwan O New Town would not have been possible without the participation of the private sector.'

Hopefully, particularly with the development of the Northern Metropolis, more developers can be encouraged to participate and embrace this philosophy in the future.

Finally, in an attempt to start educating and exposing the younger generation of Hong Kong to the concepts and value of placemaking, the Swire Properties Placemaking Academy was established in 2019. It offers all Hong Kong university students annually a rare opportunity to form a team and compete to take the lead in a six-month project designing, planning, and executing the White Christmas Street Fair, which is the company's annual year-end community celebration held in Taikoo Place. In addition to valuable hands-on experience, the students will be mentored by the company's senior management, event-planning experts, and leaders from the design and community planning industries. The 2023 edition of this event was won by HKMU students.

A special thank you to my son-in-law, Daniel J Trotter, for all his invaluable help in the preparation and organization of this manuscript to ensure it complies with all the requirements of Hong Kong University Press.

Roger Nissim

References

Burton, Mel, and Nicola Dempsey. 2012. 'Defining Placemaking: The Long-Term Management of Public Spaces'. *Urban Forestry & Urban Greening* 11:11–20.

Jacobs, Jane. 1961. *The Death and Life of Great American Cities*. New York: Random House.

U.S. Department of Arts and Culture. 2016. 'Creative Placemaking, Placekeeping, and Cultural Strategies to Resist Displacement'. https://usdac.us/blogac/2017/12/11/creative-placemaking-placekeeping-and-cultural-strategies-to-resist-displacement.

Wyckoff, Mark A. 2014. 'Four types of placemaking'. Public Square: A CNU Journal. https://www.cnu.org/publicsquare/four-types-placemaking.

Wyckoff, Mark A. 2016. *Placemaking as an Economic Development Tool: A Placemaking Guidebook*. Michigan State University. https://www.canr.msu.edu/resources/pmedtguidebook.

1

Hongkong Land's Footbridge Network in Central

Anyone who has lived and worked in Hong Kong for a number of years will likely be familiar with this intricate elevated footbridge network to the point of taking the air-conditioned convenience it provides for granted. This observation should not be taken as a criticism of the daily users, but as a compliment to the company that has, over many years, brought this network seamlessly into being as an accepted fact of life in Central.

The Evolution of This Network

This fine example of placemaking has not only been expanded to serve the wider Central District but has, just as importantly, served as a very good planning model that other districts of Hong Kong, such as north Wan Chai, Taikoo Place (see Chapter 2), the town centre developments of Sha Tin (see Chapter 5), and other new towns have been able to successfully follow.

So how, when, and why did this network start?

You need to go back to the early 1960s when the sites of Prince's Building and what is now the Mandarin Oriental Hotel (formerly Queen's Building) were being planned for redevelopment. The rather conservative general manager at the time, Bevan Field, was the lone dissenter at a Board Meeting held on 7 July 1960 who argued for the Queen's Building site to be redeveloped as an office building, which he felt would offer higher and more reliable returns. His minority view was not supported by the remainder of the Board, which was led by the rather more forward-looking Chairman, Hugh Barton, and the decision was made to proceed with the hotel scheme.

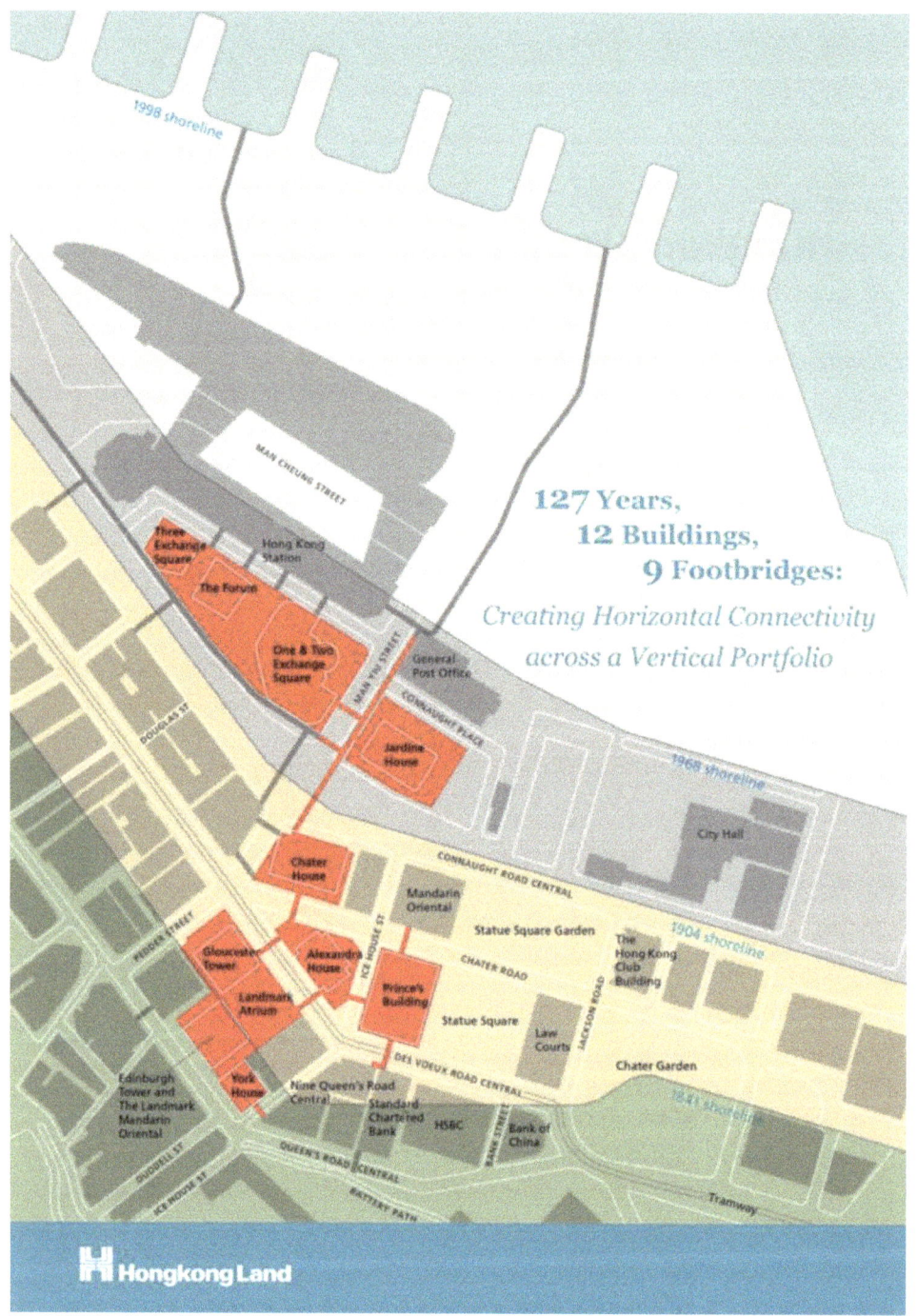

Figure 1.1: Hongkong Land: Central Footbridge Hub. Photograph courtesy of Hongkong Land.

At a board meeting held on 23 January 1961, Barton is on record as having said 'it would be a good selling point for the new hotel if an announcement could be made of the Company's intention to redevelop the northern half of Prince's Building to include a shopping centre with a connecting bridge for pedestrians between the two buildings.'

Redevelopment work proceeded and the shareholders were told at the 1963 Annual General Meeting held on 25 March of that year of Prince's Building's 'attractively designed Shopping Centre comprising 46,400 square feet (approximately 4,310 square metres) on the ground, mezzanine and first floors. The shop tenants will be selected primarily for their appeal to the needs and tastes of the guests of The Mandarin Hotel on the other side of the road . . . the Island residents, the business community and the many thousands of visiting tourists and businessmen . . . will then have a shopping centre which should vie successfully with anything that our sister city, Kowloon, has to offer.'

It was also considered necessary to introduce the then novel concept of a shopping centre in an office building. 'The Management considered it in the Company's interests to advertise the shopping centre drawing attention to its many advantages to a selected section of the public. This method of assistance to the shop tenants was to be preferred to rebating of rental in their settling-in months.'

At the end of 1963, the hotel was finished externally, the piling of Prince's Building was done, and the lower floors were progressing. There was a formal grand opening for the hotel on 25 October 1963 with then governor Sir Robert and Lady Black as well as the Duke and Duchess of Kent in attendance. But neither the mezzanine floor of shops nor the bridge to Prince's Building existed until eighteen months later.

As both buildings were under planning and development at the same time, this facilitated the internal designs of both buildings to incorporate the proposed footbridge as well as the circulation routes to the main office and hotel lift lobbies, retail levels, and down to street level entries. Locating escalators and stairs now became much more important.

Thus, two new concepts were introduced that would have a major influence on Hongkong Land's future planning, development, and redevelopment of their Central portfolio: mixed-use retail and office buildings with interlinking pedestrian footbridges.

The next significant footbridge link came along when Hongkong Land bought the site of what was initially called Connaught Centre, now named Jardine House. This was at a government auction in 1970 for a reclamation site north of Connaught Road Central. At the time, the site was considered to be relatively isolated, so the land lease stipulated that the successful purchaser must build a footbridge across Connaught Road Central to link into the old Union House (also known as Swire House), now redeveloped as Chater House.

To the south of Connaught Road Central , Hongkong Land were in a unique position as they owned a significant number of commercial buildings directly adjacent to each other separated by just three roads; Chater Road, Des Voeux Road and Ice House Street. Therefore, they were able to plan and implement this as yet untried concept of connecting adjacent

Figure 1.2: First footbridge across Chater Road, completed 1963. Photograph courtesy of Hongkong Land.

Figure 1.3: Exchange Square. Photograph courtesy of Hongkong Land.

Figure 1.4: Landmark Building. Photograph courtesy of Hongkong Land.

Figure 1.5: Alexandra House to Landmark. Photograph courtesy of Hongkong Land.

buildings by an innovative footbridge network without the need to obtain the approval or consent of other owners which, at that time, might have been a long and possibly fruitless endeavour!

The early success of the first footbridges meant that the concept was to feature strongly in Hongkong Land's master plan that was presented to the government in December 1973, which was to reshape the heart of the Central Business District through its programme of demolishing and redeveloping its existing portfolio of buildings. The first phase, involving the redevelopment of the 20-storey Alexandra House into its larger 36-storey successor, was followed by the demolition of five old Hongkong Land buildings to make way for the mammoth Landmark complex. Between 1978 and 1983, the company joined the new Alexandra House, which, by virtue of its central position within the portfolio, became the 'hub' of Central's footbridge network, with four connections radiating out to Prince's Building, Swire House (which on redevelopment in 2002 became Chater House), and the Landmark complex. Further connections were added upon the completion of Exchange Square Towers One and Two in 1985.

At this point, the concept launched by Hongkong Land was compelling enough that owners of neighbouring buildings saw value in linking their properties to this footbridge network. Between 1985 and 1990, extensions followed to the adjoining Central Building, across Queen's Road Central to Central Tower, and then across Wyndham Street into the Entertainment Building. By 1990, a Hongkong Land footbridge from Prince's Building was built into the new Standard Chartered Bank Building, further extended into the HSBC headquarters, and then further over Queen's Road Central to Battery Path. The main 'ring' in Central was finally complete when Hongkong Land constructed a footbridge across Ice House Street to link their newly completed Nine Queen's Road Central to The Landmark.

The 2003 redevelopment of the Alexandra House retail podium enabled the existing first floor podium walkways to be removed. Hongkong Land were able to take advantage of the Building (Planning) Regulations, which specifically enable the Building Authority to grant bonus gross floor area in return for areas within private developments being dedicated to and allowing 24-hour access for public passage. In this case, Hongkong Land were granted an additional 5,200 square metres of developable area, which was translated into an additional floor of retail as part of the major renovations.

The same 'win-win' formula was repeated for The Landmark refurbishment scheme from 2003–2007. This again incorporated internal 24-hour dedicated public passageways and a new vehicular drop-off on Queen's Road Central, linked by numerous escalators to the footbridge levels as well as to the existing basement level Mass Transit Railway Corporation (MTRC) connections.

The major re-configuration of the retail podiums of Alexandra House and The Landmark enabled the re-examination of the potential of these two premises in terms of both development and architectural design. In both cases, the opportunity to reconfigure the internal circulation pattern was explored, to the extent that major structural alterations were carried out to create new voids, readjust floor levels, rearrange escalators, and extensively reshuffle tenant spaces.

Placekeeping

The Hongkong Land footbridge network is now well over fifty years old, having existed since the opening of the first bridge in 1965. For the first half of their existence these footbridges were mainly regarded as functional; that is to say, to permit pedestrians to walk from one building to another in comparative convenience and safety. From the late 1980s through the 1990s, with the exception of the footbridge across Connaught Road Central, there was a programme to fully enclose and air condition the network which coincided with the globalisation of retail branding and commercial office tenants' demands for a more sophisticated working environment. What was happening was that the footbridge network had evolved well beyond its original remit and now acted as a seamless extension to the traditional office lobby and retail mall, to the point where there is no longer any distinction between building and footbridge, as the two have become totally integrated. They are now recognized for more than their convenience value, possessing an actual commercial value with some opportunities for branding and exhibitions. Their planning and interior design are treated no differently to the office lobbies and retail malls to which they connect. These continuous upgrading activities are all related to the importance of not only providing the quality 'placemaking' in the first place, but also of retaining that quality through a vigorous ongoing programme of upgrades that can, rightly, be called 'placekeeping'.

A good example of this is the relatively recent completion of the redevelopment of The Forum in 2014, which has revitalised this area by providing a contemporary, well designed, disabled access to the public open space. This has become an important pedestrian hub providing convenient connections between the Central elevated walkway network and their Exchange Square developments, International Finance Centre, and the Airport Express Hong Kong Station.

Another element of this place keeping is Hongkong Land's long track record of installing public artworks throughout its Central portfolio, including the footbridge network and associated open spaces. Perhaps the best examples are the two semi-abstract bronze pieces which they commissioned from the world-famous sculptor, the late Henry Moore, in the mid-1970s; 'Double Oval' is now sited at the entrance to Jardine House and 'Oval with Points' sits outside the entrance to Exchange Square.

Since Two Exchange Square was completed in 1985, 'The Rotunda' was opened and has become a venue for public exhibition programmes of artworks as well as a venue for organizations like the American Institute of Architects to hold their annual award-winning presentations.

Hongkong Land's Footbridge Network in Central

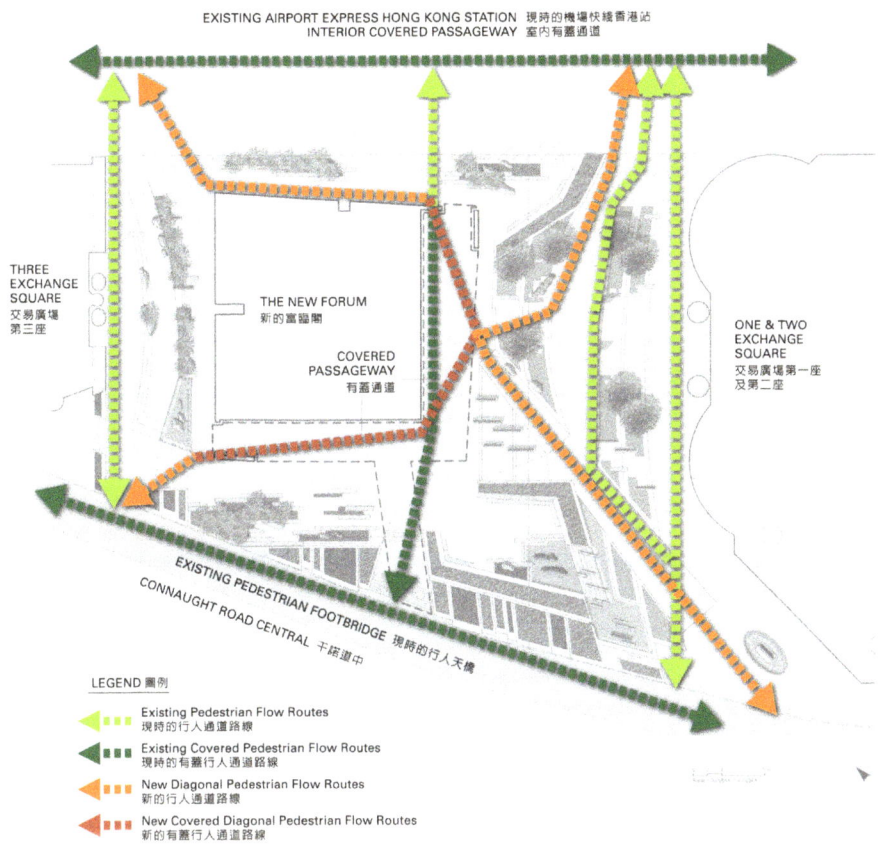

Figure 1.6: New Forum layout. Photograph courtesy of Hongkong Land.

During a 2014 interview with the US based non-profit organisation Council on Tall Buildings and Urban Habitat (CTBUH), the former Executive Director of Hongkong Land, James Robinson, was asked: 'Have you determined how much value footbridges bring to a project?' He answered: 'It's a hard number to determine, but putting in the footbridges and allowing retail to expand both vertically and horizontally across buildings has driven enough traffic that it now comprises around 25% of our total annual retail profits in Hong Kong.'

Central's elevated footbridge network, together with other examples on Hong Kong Island, Kowloon, and the New Towns in the New Territories, can now be considered as a fixture in twentieth-first-century urban design and planning policy. The network extends seven kilometres across forty buildings, with the government adding to the networks' value by providing connections to public parks and pedestrianized zones, allowing car-free pedestrian

Figure 1.7: Henry Moore 1968 sculpture, Oval with Points, Exchange Square. Photograph courtesy of Hongkong Land.

movement from Admiralty to Sheung Wan, and to the Central-mid-level Escalator System and MTR. The success of the system demonstrates the importance of cooperation between developers, property owners, and the government.

The up-to-date (2020) map reproduced below was sourced from Hongkong Land, Google Maps, A521jgh89, redrawn by CTBUH, and clearly shows the full extent of this network with the Hongkong Land footbridges forming the central hub.

Government Contribution

The government's major contribution was the issuing of the Principal Licensing Agreement on 7 September 1990, followed by a Supplementary Licence Agreement dated 12 November 2004 to give the necessary consents where any of the footbridge network cross public roads. Reference is made in the preamble of the Principal Licensing Agreement to the first licence agreement dated 8 September 1972, when the then governor granted Hongkong Land the permission to construct, operate, and maintain an integrated network of interconnected elevated pedestrian passageways, stairways, and bridges crossing various parts of the Central District, Hong Kong, called the Network for short. Over time, there were necessary

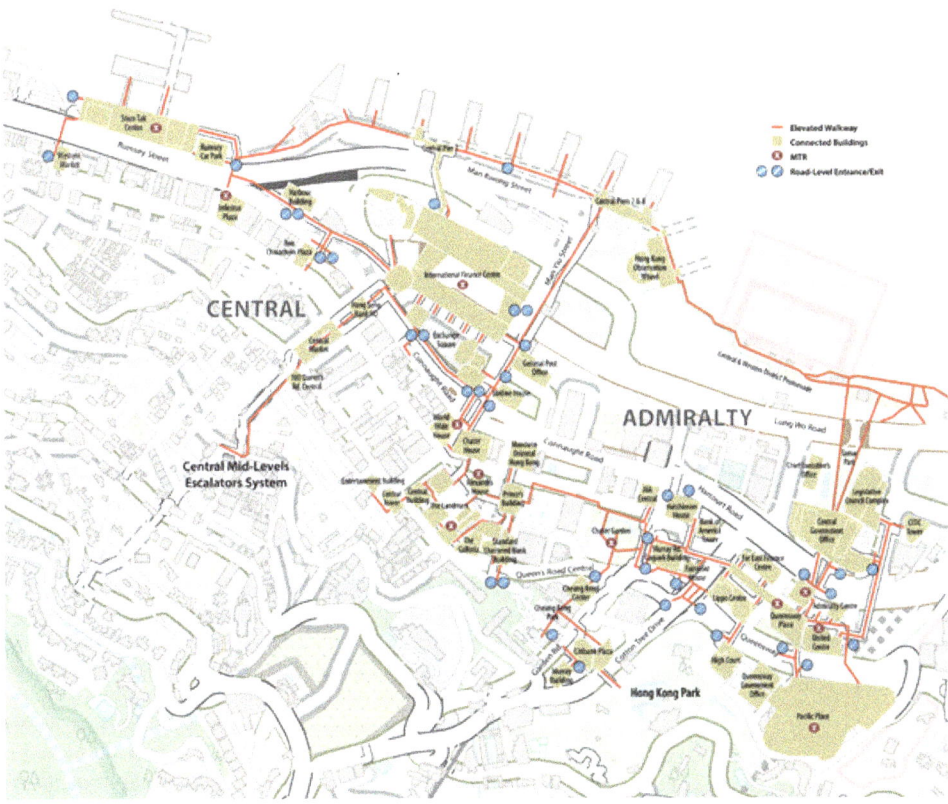

Figure 1.8: Central's entire elevated footbridge network—drawn by the CTBUH. Illustration courtesy of Hongkong Land.

amendments and additions to the Network with, for example, the development of Exchange Square, the redevelopment of Chater House, and the refurbishment of Alexandra House, which are now covered by the Supplementary Licence Agreement.

In return for the government granting the right and permission to operate, repair, maintain, and uphold the Network in its present position, Hongkong Land, as the licensee, has to perform and observe the following key conditions and stipulations:

1. Repair and maintain the Network to render it safe and suitable for public pedestrian use. Such works must be carried out in all respects in compliance with the Buildings Ordinance.

2. With very few exceptions, the licensee shall allow access to and shall keep open for use by the public as a pedestrian thoroughfare, free from obstruction, and free of cost. Where the Network passes through private buildings, for security reasons, opening hours are reduced.
3. The Network shall be used solely for the passage on foot of members of the general public, tenants, occupiers, and licensees of the Licensee.
4. The Network shall not be used for commercial purposes except for most parts of the Network the display of advertising internally is permissible. External advertising is not permitted.
5. Utility services as required to serve the Network are permitted and additional services may be allowed with written consent.

As can be seen, the government, recognizing the huge public benefits this Network provides, has been a willing partner and facilitator of this project right from the early days in 1972.

Today, these footbridges are now subject to contemporary requirements for disabled access and fire suppression (sprinkler) systems to help contain the spread of fire from one building to another.

In summary, the overall urban benefits they confer, for both the public and the private property owners, are largely self-evident and cannot be overstated.

For the public, they are free and include:

- Diminished pedestrian congestion at ground level
- Increased pedestrian mobility
- Improved pedestrian environment
- Improved pedestrian safety and security
- Opportunities for easy access to gardens, MTR, transport interchanges, and greening of the roofs

For the property owners, they fairly reflect the costs of construction and ongoing management and maintenance and include:

- The potential for overlap and connection of functions between buildings
- Effectively giving an additional floor of prime retail – for example, because of the connectivity of the first floors of Alexandra House and Chater House, the second of the Landmark became more accessible as if it was a ground floor retail mall
- The use of the network for permitted services, where appropriate

Concluding Comments

The most recent words, which further justify this network as correctly being described as 'place making', come from visiting Italian architect and academic Pina (Giusi) Cioteli, whose essay entitled 'Urban hyper-connections of Hong Kong. Towards a Vertical Fabric for the contemporary metropolis' was published in the *Hong Kong Institute of Architects* (HKIA) *Journal* (Cioteli 2019). Here are some extracts: 'As a place where vertical buildings, malls, and meeting spaces all link to the public pedestrian system, Hong Kong can be considered the most complete example of vertical fabric at an urban scale to date.' Writing about the Central Elevated Walkway cluster, Leslie Lu (2005) observed that it created a new infrastructure system that has evolved into 'a distinct and separate pedestrian network, linking existing landmarks and creating a new urban locus. Although this development points out the virtual abandonment of the street, the network of elevated walkways created a new urban configuration of Hong Kong: it became the "new ground" of the city, reorganizing flow with new connections, indifferent to existing urban patterns. For these reasons, Hong Kong is an emblematic case study to examine the transformation of a commercial fabric into a vertical – and volumetric – one.'

Acknowledgements

I very much appreciate the positive and significant inputs into the history and background of the evolution of this network by former Hongkong Land executive director, Jim Robinson and former Hongkong Land communications consultant Martin Spurrier, who were both closely involved with the developments and redevelopments described above.

References

Cioteli, Pina Giusi. 2019. 'Urban Hyper-connections of Hong Kong. Towards a Vertical Fabric for the Contemporary Metropolis.' *HKIA Journal* 75 (2019): 41–43.

Lu, Leslie. 2005. 'The Asia Arcades Project: Progressive Porosity'. *Perspecta* 36: 88–89.

Hongkong Land's Footbridge Network in Central: Commentary (NC)

An extensive network of elevated pedestrian walkways in the Central business district has unfolded over the decades since the first footbridge to link the Mandarin Oriental Hotel and Prince's Building over Chater Road in 1965. From initial point-to-point connections, this network of pedestrian footbridges developed by Hongkong Land has expanded to define and make an identifiable place in the city.

In fact, the first notion of linking commercial buildings in Central with elevated walkways dates back much earlier to 1927, when the developer, originally Jardine Matheson & Co., first considered to connect the former King's and York Buildings on the Praya Central with a footbridge. However, this scheme was abandoned when estimated construction costs exceeded the original budget by over 50% (Mo 2017).

Subsequent plans were also considered, but not realised, in the 1950s to connect various commercial buildings, including the former Union House and an earlier generation of Alexandra House, by projecting canopies above ground floor footpaths as elevated walkways acting as 'first floor pavements . . . connected to similar structures on adjacent buildings and could be continued across streets as to form a continuous pedestrian level' (The New Union House 1958).

Enclosed footbridges – also referred to as skywalks or skyways – became popular in North America, especially in cities with severe winters. Perhaps most notably, the Minneapolis Skyway System has interconnected eighty urban blocks with eighteen kilometres of pedestrian bridges in downtown Minneapolis since the mid-1960s.

More recently, the High Line in New York City was completed in 2019 after converting an obsolete stretch of elevated railway (2.3 kilometres) into a linear urban park.

In this instance, the pedestrian skyway is outdoors, not enclosed; a public enterprise, not private; and building on existing infrastructure, not a new structure. As a placemaker, the High Line has not only created a new tourist destination but also spurred real estate development in this former industrial district on the West Side of Manhattan.

Beyond connectivity, placemaking requires the physical interaction of people, space, and activities. In contrast to the winters of North America, the summers of Hong Kong need protection from heat and humidity; thus, the Central footbridges are enclosed with air conditioning to offer both convenience and comfort while seamlessly extending the outlook and activities of refined lobbies and arcades on either end, not merely utilitarian linkages. While the property developer is naturally motivated by private, commercial interests to promote foot traffic by retail customers to its upper-level shopping arcades, the long-term consequence has been public, civic benefits for everyone else – office workers, residents, and tourists alike – with ease of accessibility safely above the hustle and bustle of the congested city streets below. With a second layer of elevated pedestrian walkways stitched into the urban fabric, individual blocks of the Hongkong Land portfolio in Central have been interwoven and transformed into an identifiable place within its vertical city.

Key Notes

1. Private commercial interests can lead to public civic benefits.
2. Pedestrian network has evolved into an identifiable place.
3. Vertical dimension of placemaking in the urban fabric.

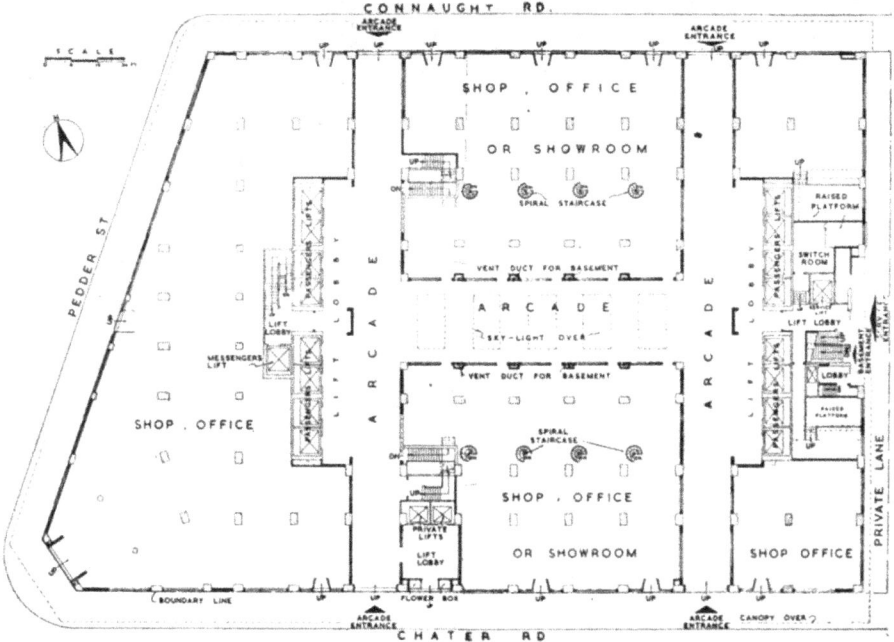

Ground floor plan showing the positions of lifts and stairways etc. Phase 2 will be the western portion of the building including the west arcade.

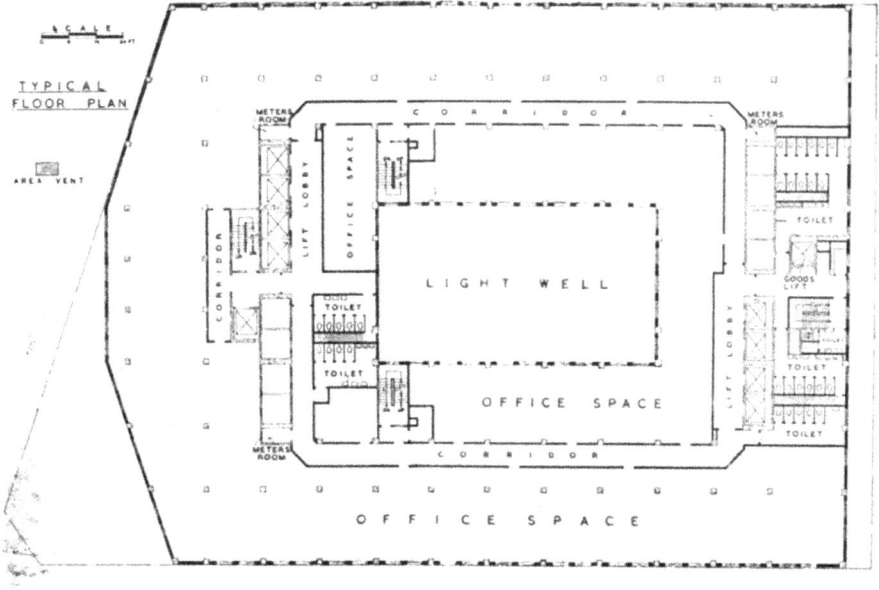

Figure 1.9: Plan and image of building connections, 1958. Illustration from *Hong Kong and Far East Builder*.

Figure 1.10: Elevated walkway in Central at The Landmark, Hong Kong. Photograph courtesy of Hongkong Land.

References

Mo, Kar Him. 2017. 'Profit, Virtue and Megaform: Hongkong Land's Building Activities in Central District, 1889–1983.' PhD diss., The Chinese University of Hong Kong. http://repository.lib.cuhk.edu.hk/en/item/cuhk-1587286.

'The New Union House.' 1958. *Hong Kong and Far East Builder* 13 (5): 7–9. https://digitalrepository.lib.hku.hk/catalog/lr66pv492.

2

Swire Properties: Taikoo Place

A Little Bit of History

On the site of Taikoo Place originally stood the Taikoo Sugar Refinery which, when completed in 1884, was one of the largest and most sophisticated plants in the world.

The refinery ceased operation in 1972 and was refurbished as a warehouse and office; much of it was leased to the Longman Group (Far East) Ltd. It was demolished in the late 1980s and redeveloped into Hong Kong Telecom Tower (now PCCW Tower) and Dorset House.

Next door is Taikoo Shing where originally stood the Taikoo Dockyard, completed in 1907, for repairing and building ships.

Shipbuilding had ceased by 1970 and the repairing part of the business was, in 1973, combined in a joint venture with Hutchison Whampoa to form Hong Kong United Dockyard. They first merged their dockyard operations onto a site on Tsing Yi Island in 1980. Their new modern facility, capable of handling large, modern day container ships, is also located on Tsing Yi Island and was completed in 1990. Swire Properties, which was established in 1972, were thus able to demolish the old dockyard in phases as the transition to Tsing Yi took place; this allowed the continued construction of Taikoo Shing, which had already started on land at Tsui Woo Terrace. The first master layout plan for Taikoo Shing was approved in early 1974 and the first phase of this 61-block housing estate, which would deliver 12,690 apartments by 1987, was started in 1975 with pre-sales the following year.

One important point to remember is that the land leases of both the sugar refinery and the dockyard were granted for 999 years from 1882 and 1900 respectively and were virtually unrestricted as to user giving the owners considerable flexibility as to how and when they

Figure 2.1: Taikoo Sugar Refinery, 1884. Photograph courtesy of Swire Properties.

Figure 2.2: Taikoo Dockyard, 1907. Photograph courtesy of Swire Properties.

could be developed and redeveloped. The combined area of these adjoining sites amounts to 1.1 million square feet (approximately 102,200 square metres).

The interrelationship between the two developments is also significant as, in simple terms, the large revenues generated in the years following the ongoing development and sale of the flats in Taikoo Shing meant that Swire Properties had a sufficiently strong cash flow that enabled them to finance the building of Taikoo Place. The elderly Jock Swire, although personally not enamoured by either Hong Kong or the redevelopment project, is reported as saying after one of his periodic visits in 1973: 'It's money, money, money all the way!'

Another point to remember is that the holding company, John Swire & Sons, remains to this day a privately owned company in which the majority shareholding remains with the Swire family, retaining a strong influence on the future direction the company takes. A good example is the positive response the family had to the signing of the Sino-British Joint Declaration on 19 December 1984, which set out the future for Hong Kong post-1997. They were, quite probably, encouraged by the wording of paragraph 1 of Annex III, which relates solely to land leases. It states that all leases granted or decided upon before the entry into force of the Sino-British Joint Declaration, which would include their precious 999-year leases, would have all their rights recognized and protected by law. The decision was therefore made to stay and invest in Hong Kong and they gave strategic support committing to significant new developments such as Pacific Place and Taikoo Place.

Taikoo Place Starts to Take Shape

Between 1979 and 1988 the first generation of new buildings came on stream. Warwick House was completed in 1979, Cornwall House in 1984, and Somerset House was opened in 1988. These buildings were relatively low rise as a result of height limits imposed due to their proximity to the former Kai Tak airport. In order to capture the permitted gross floor area, they maximized their site coverage with large floor plates on the lower floors suitable for light industrial, warehouse, or godown use and the upper floors suitable for related ancillary offices. Over time, the demand for this space shifted to back office and lower rent users such as architects and designers. Technology then became a serious focus after signing HK Telecom, which was Hong Kong's largest company by market cap in 1992. The advent of the internet 'bubble' of 1998–2000 resulted in those types of companies replacing the light industry and warehouse users, as the expansive floor plate and heavy floor loading meant the space was highly suitable for use as data centres such that these buildings could then be labelled as 'techno centres'.

Figure 2.3: Warwick House. Photograph courtesy of Swire Properties.

Figure 2.4: Taikoo Place. Photograph courtesy of Swire Properties.

Connectivity to this location was greatly enhanced when the Island Eastern Corridor was opened in 1984 and the Mass Transit Railway (MTR) Island Line opened in the following year. This very much upgraded accessibility resulted in these techno-centres attracting a wider range of higher value end users. More importantly, because of the enhanced connectivity to the traditional central business district (CBD), it helped start the decentralisation movement that brought a significant number of office-based businesses to Island East. In 1990 the sites were rezoned as a 'comprehensive development area' which prompted the change in name from Taikoo Trading Estate to Taikoo Place. The transition to purely office developments followed, starting from west to east. Those with the better access to the MTR came first, with Devon House opening in 1993, Dorset House and PCCW Tower completed in 1994; Lincoln House opened in 1998, Oxford House in 1999, and Cambridge House in 2003.

During the 1990s Swire Properties had patiently acquired the vast majority of the undivided shares in two immediately adjoining industrial buildings, Melbourne Building and Aik San Building, whose sites were zoned for commercial use on the Quarry Bay Outline Zoning Plan. Frustrated by the unreasonableness of the last remaining owner, Swire Properties were the first company to successfully make use of the Land (Compulsory Sale for Redevelopment) Ordinance (Cap. 545). Enacted in 1999, the ordinance's purpose was to assist developers who had already obtained at least 90% (later lowered to 80%) of a property's interests to complete the acquisition of 100% of all the interests in order to facilitate redevelopment which, in this case, occurred in 2002. This was vitally important as the sites were to be developed as One Island East.

The demand for good quality decentralized offices had continued to gather pace in the late 1980s and early 1990s when it became clear that the top-quality tenants such as banks, investment houses, lawyers, and others were looking for Grade A offices with a floor plate of between 20–25,000 gross square feet (approximately 1,850–2,320 square metres). Supply for this grade and size of office was very limited in Central, so this gave Swire Properties the perfect opportunity to fill the gap in supply at Taikoo Place.

The iconic One Island East was completed in 2008 and met the new standard, followed by Swire Properties' first triple Grade-A office tower, One Taikoo Place, completed in 2018 and Two Taikoo Place in 2022.

In order to achieve this grading, the latter two office towers were built in accordance with the Company's vision to become the leading sustainable development performer in its industry by 2030; they achieved the highest sustainability standards of Platinum LEED BD+C: Core and Shell Version 2009 as well as Platinum HK BEAM Plus New Buildings Version 1.2 green building standards. The third certification comes from the WELL Building Standard, which is third-party certified by the Green Business Certification Incorporated, an organization that also administers the LEED certification and which measures and evaluates the indoor parameters that will affect the health and well-being of the building's occupants, that is to say 'human sustainability'.

In 2014 the HK$15 billion Taikoo Place Redevelopment project was started to progressively redevelop the old techno-centres mentioned above; this was substantially completed in September 2022 with the opening of Two Taikoo Place, their second triple Grade A office tower, Taikoo Square, and Taikoo Garden. Although the techno-centres were still relatively new and developed to the maximum plot ratio, their height restrictions, layout, and design were not suitable for today's office space demands; their redevelopment, without the need for any lease modification or premium, made economic sense as the higher rents achievable for a triple Grade-A office justified the decision to demolish and rebuild.

The completion of One Island East saw the perception of Taikoo Place change from being not just a decentralized office location but a credible, first choice alternative to Central, given the specification (spec) of the accommodation it offered compared to the older office buildings in Central. The basic value proposition was 'twice the spec at half the cost'. The banking sector and certain professional services, specifically accountants, were using One Island East for back and middle office functions, but it was the relocation of Freshfields (the first 'magic circle' law firm) that was the catalyst for other law firms to move down to Taikoo Place. Until then it was more insurance companies and technology, media, and telecom tenants that had their head office located here.

Figure 2.5: One Island East and Taikoo Place. Photograph courtesy of Swire Properties.

Figure 2.6: Taikoo Park. Photograph courtesy of Swire Properties.

With Two Taikoo Place now completed, Taikoo Place will be well placed to qualify as Hong Kong's second global business district after Central, not just based on the spec of the accommodation but based on the surrounding environment and amenity provision. These are commensurate, if not better than, Central (Ernst & Young and ULI 2020). A review of the Taikoo Place masterplan shows a well-thought-out layout with the individual office blocks each having space around them for light and ventilation. The disposition of the gardens, squares, and parks are also well distributed with convenient access provided both at

Figure 2.7: Two Taikoo Place. Photograph courtesy of Swire Properties.

grade and by the first-floor air-conditioned elevated footbridges that ensure a peaceful and tranquil environment for both the office workers and public visitors, a noticeable contrast to the more frenetic atmosphere of the CBD in Central. See Figure 2.10 below.

One Island East was completed in 2008 and stands 301 metres high, the tallest building in Taikoo Place. At the time the building was designed and approved under the 2003 Quarry Bay Outline Zoning Plan, there were no restrictions on plot ratio or height on the site, which was zoned for commercial use. In order to achieve the necessary floor space and height they wanted, Swire Properties included the site area of what is now Taikoo Park, which at the time was zoned for commercial and residential use, in the development area calculations. This land formed part of their 999-year leasehold land holdings and so was highly valuable; nevertheless, the intention was always to develop this portion of the development site as a garden for the benefit of the local community. In other words, it was a positive bit of placemaking. In

Figure 2.8: Taikoo Square. Photograph courtesy of Swire Properties.

2010, through the new Quarry Bay Outline Zoning Plan, the Planning Department – somewhat belatedly – decided that they needed to impose building height controls to preserve the views to the ridge lines from the waterfront promenade. They have now imposed a 220-metre height limit on any future redevelopment of the One Island East site. This comes a bit late in the day, since this high-quality building should last for up to one hundred years – something of a pyrrhic victory for the planners! At the same time, the site of Taikoo Park was zoned as open space even though the land remained in private ownership; in effect, privatizing such provision. The sites of both Taikoo Garden and Taikoo Square, designed by the award-winning London-based landscape architecture practice Gustafson Porter + Bowman (famed for the Diana, Princess of Wales Memorial Fountain in Hyde Park, London), have created high-quality, privately managed, public spaces all as part of the Taikoo Place masterplan.

In total, over 300 multinational corporations, including many Fortune 500 companies, from banking and finance, legal services, insurance, accounting, luxury brands, consulting, media and advertising services, digital communications, and technology are tenants here. There are more than 30,000 office workers within this portfolio which, with the completion of Two Taikoo Place in September 2022, now comprises ten office towers with over 7.1 million square feet (approximately 660,000 square metres) of space with virtually 100% occupancy.

With the recently completed Central-Wanchai Bypass and the Island Eastern Corridor link in operation, Taikoo Place is now only minutes away by road from Causeway Bay and Central and half an hour from the airport. This has helped further to drive the decentralization movement and has brought a significant number of office-based businesses to Island East. By the end of 2018, Island East accounted for about 7% of Grade-A offices in Hong Kong. Of the additional Grade-A office space built since 2000, Island East accounts for about 10%.

Placemaking and Placekeeping

The Swire Properties Annual Report 2022 sets out their Sustainable Development 2030 (SD2030) Strategy in which they state: 'Through effective placemaking and long-term placekeeping, we aim to continue to transform the places in which we invest so as to create value whilst retaining their character, supporting communities, and enhancing people's lives.'

In fact, the Swire Group have a long history and tradition of both placemaking and placekeeping going back to the very early days when the sugar refinery and shipyard were built. By 1893, the refinery employed nearly 2,000 Chinese workers and by 1912, the dockyard employed some 4,000 workers. Although the Hongkong Tramway opened in 1904, this was still a relatively remote location, so the need to provide staff living quarters was obvious. By 1910, housing units for 4,000 people were built together with a clinic and hospital, cinema, canteen, and recreation grounds, creating what was called a 'Native Village' (Bickers 2020, 134, 186, 188, 243). In 1923, they opened a free school for the children of their workers in the refinery and dockyard that became the predecessor to Taikoo Primary School.

Figure 2.9: Taikoo Chinese School, circa 1950. Photograph courtesy of Swire Properties.

This high level of care and attention for their workers has, today, now been transferred to and enjoyed by their tenants!

Today, these tenants can enjoy a wide range of business and leisure amenities in the area, including EAST residences and the unique multi-purpose venue for visual and performing arts called ArtisTree, which opened in 2008 in Cornwall House. In 2017, Blueprint was relaunched, offering a premium co-working hub with flexible workspace and a full range of dedicated, state-of-the-art, event space. There is a new private members' club available called

The Refinery, which replaced the former Butterfield's, and within five minutes' walk there is the business hotel EAST Hong Kong and the shopping and restaurant complex of Cityplaza. The office workers are also catered for as the tenant mix of restaurants and food outlets are designed to give a wide range of affordable lunch, coffee, and snack options.

Similar to the elevated footbridge network in Central, the Paris-based design company Hugh Dutton Associes was commissioned to design the extended portion of the elevated walkway system and seamlessly link all the various office towers in Taikoo Place with a comprehensive barrier-free, climate-controlled network of footbridges which span from One Island East nearly all the way to Quarry Bay MTR station. Apart from the final bridge that connects King's Road to Devon House, all the other bridges are, in effect, private bridges because they span the internal service roads which sit on the land owned by Swire Properties, giving them flexibility as to their size, location, and use. In addition to their connectivity function, they also provide an important linking and unifying function to all the office towers and open spaces within the portfolio for the benefit of both the office community as well as the visiting public.

An appreciation of this system appeared in a chapter of the book *The City at Eye Level Asia* entitled 'Creating New Layers of Public Space Through Elevated Walkways' (van Steekelenburg 2019, 206–7). The opening words observed that 'by creating one of the largest privately owned walking systems in the region, Swire Properties had been able to make a bold place statement. Taikoo Place's system of walking bridges has created an additional layer of public space to the city's urban jungle, an air-conditioned alternative to street level. The ingenious planning solution is also tailored to the context of Hong Kong where real estate is more expensive than almost any other place in the world and public spaces come at a premium.'

Another important distinguishing feature is the ground level 'sense of arrival' with dedicated weather protected drop off points for vehicular traffic, as well as for pedestrian traffic through landscaped areas lined by retail.

As part of their ongoing and constantly evolving placekeeping function, Swire Properties organised events and activities during 2018 and 2019 (pre-COVID) that were attended by more than 440,000 people and that included world-class and innovative arts at ArtisTree. Together with their flagship tenant engagement programme, Project After 6, this all helped reinforce Taikoo Place as a vibrant and dynamic office hub. With the effects of COVID now receding, their hard work has brought attendance back up to pre-COVID figures.

In addition, on its completion in 2024 Taikoo Square and Taikoo Garden are able to provide nearly 70,000 square feet (6,500 square metres) of open space for the whole community to enjoy, with stunning water features, lush greenery, and quiet pathways.

In 2015, the Tong Chong Street Market was launched and had grown into a popular weekly event, taking place on Sunday's, selling fresh locally produced foods grown by local farmers. The market is yet to reopen post-COVID, pending the completion of the upgrading of Tong Chong Street.

In addition to supporting local Hong Kong farmers, the market aims to engage Swire Properties employees, tenants, and neighbours on the importance of food cycles and sustainable production. On the same theme, Swire Properties have developed a sustainable exhibition centre called The Loop not only to increase environmental awareness but also to showcase their environmental initiatives and their historical connections to the area.

Chairman Guy Bradley anticipates that in the post-COVID-19 world the market will place an even higher emphasis on the quality of the environment with demands for more energy efficiency and state of the art environmental features, which he is confident his company's buildings will continue to be able to offer. According to the 2022 Annual Report, the occupancy rates at One Taikoo Place, One Island East and other offices in Taikoo Place were 100%, 96%, and 95% let respectively as at 31 December 2022, demonstrating that even during those difficult and challenging times the company was reaping the rewards for its high-quality placemaking and placekeeping during this redevelopment program.

Finally, Bradley has laid down a strong goal for his team moving forward by saying 'Our vision is to be the leading sustainable development performer in our industry globally by 2030.' This vision was codified in their SD2030 strategy in 2016–2017 and the steps for achieving this ambitious goal were set out by the company in their March 2020 Places Impact Report 'The Creative Transformation of Island East and Development of Taikoo Place'.

Key Notes

1. Conversations in May 2020 with Keith Kerr, former CEO 1 March 1989–31 May 2009 and Guy Bradley, the CEO from 1 January 2015, and who was elected chairman on 25 August 2021.
2. All images kindly provided by Swire Properties.

References

Bickers, Robert. 2020. *China Bound: John Swire & Sons and Its World, 1816–1980*. Bloomsbury.

Ernst & Young, and the Urban Land Institute (ULI). 2020. 'The Attractiveness of Global Business District Report: The Challenge to Remain Competitive.' Archived June 20, 2024 at https://web.archive.org/web/20240620212254/https://assets.ey.com/content/dam/ey-sites/ey-com/en_gl/topics/real-estate-hospitality-and-construction/ey-the-attractiveness-of-global-business-districts-report.pdf.

van Steekelenburg, Ester. 2019. 'Creating New Layers of Public Space through Elevated Walkways.' *The City at Eye Level Asia* (June): 206–7.

Taikoo Place: Commentary (NC)

In historical texts on buildings and cities, the lasting achievements of architects and urban planners are widely acknowledged. But, arguably, the leading influencers in shaping modern cities are property developers – especially in a metropolis such as Hong Kong, which boasts ten of the largest real estate companies among the world's Top 100 (McClary 2020).

While motivated by maximising development potential, gross floor area, and profit margins, leading developers also appreciate the need to provide public space, even if privately owned and managed. Among them, Swire Properties are widely recognised for developing high quality real estate projects including Taikoo Place (mixed-use commercial) alongside the neighbouring Cityplaza (retail) and Taikoo Shing (residential) developments that were built in succession over the past decades.

Developed in stages since the 1990s, Taikoo Place is interconnected by indoor concourses and enclosed footbridges to create an elevated pedestrian network which serves the entire community for ease of access to the MTR system while avoiding the congestion of ground level traffic including heavy vehicles. Selected bridge links are graciously apportioned to host art exhibitions and other displays, thus serving not just as passages but also as places for public activities.

At ground level, Tong Chong Street is pedestrianised. A 1.6-hectare landscaped open plaza named Taikoo Park, which has green space and water features in front of One Island East, is situated at the transition zone between the commercial (Taikoo Place) and residential (Taikoo Shing) developments. The later additions of Taikoo Square and Taikoo Garden provide further green space of 0.6 hectares to the complex.

While these total land areas are not significantly large in the context of Hong Kong, they offer precious green oases in the concrete jungle of high-rise developments. Residents of Hong Kong enjoy less than half as much open space per person than those in other Asian major cities: less than 2.8 square metres per person in Hong Kong versus 5.8–7.6 square metres per person in Tokyo, Seoul, Singapore, and Shanghai (Lai 2017). For comparison further afield: 13.5 square metres per person in New York City (Geotab 2019) and 32 square metres per person in London (Statista 2018).

The environmental, health, and social benefits of open space, especially green open space, are extensively researched and widely understood. In the high-rise, high-density urban conditions that define Hong Kong, public open spaces that are strategically located and well-designed are essential to the wellbeing of communities and identity of the city. The commitment by civic-minded developers to both the placemaking and placekeeping of privately-owned public spaces can be seen as a vital contribution.

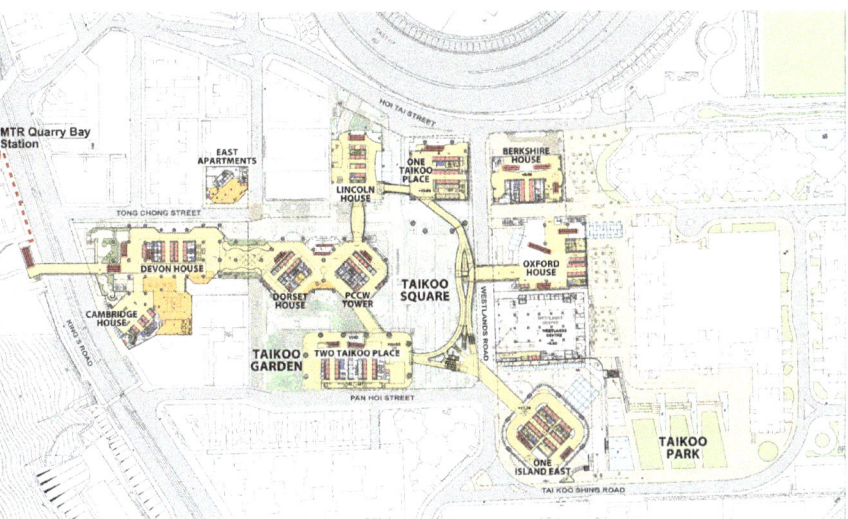 

Figure 2.10: Left: Taikoo Place Plan at footbridge level. Courtesy of Swire Properties Ltd., Wong & Ouyang (HK) Ltd. Right: Landscape Plan. Courtesy of Gustafson Porter + Bowman, Urbis Ltd., Swire Properties Ltd.

Key Notes

1. Leading role of property developers in shaping the city.
2. Privately owned and managed public spaces by civic-minded developers.
3. Place making both indoors (protected circulation) and outdoors (open green spaces).

References

Geotab. 2019. 'The Allocation of Space in U.S. Cities.' https://www.geotab.com/urban-footprint/.

Lai, Carine. 2017. 'Unopened Space: Mapping Equitable Availability of Open Space in Hong Kong'. Civic Exchange, Hong Kong. https://civic-exchange.org/report/unopened-space-mapping-equitable-availability-of-open-space-in-hong-kong/.

McClary, Samantha. 2020. 'EG Global 100: World's Biggest Real Estate-owning Companies Revealed.' https://www.egi.co.uk/news/the-top-100-global-real-estate%E2%80%91owning-companies/.

Statista. 2018. 'Green Space per Inhabitant in the City of London in the United Kingdom (UK) in 2018, by Category.' https://www.statista.com/statistics/860684/green-areas-per-inhabitant-in-london-in-the-united-kingdom/.

3

Twin Towers: Gateway Entry into Victoria Harbour

Introduction

With the completion of the International Commercial Centre (ICC) in March 2010, the 484-metre-tall tower standing on the Kowloon side of Victoria Harbour mirrored the Hong Kong Island's Two International Finance Centre (Two IFC) on the opposite south bank, which was completed in October 2003 and stands at 412 metres. Together they have become a very special and dramatic maritime western entrance to Victoria Harbour, thus providing a new symbol of Hong Kong. It is often referred to as the Victoria Harbour Gateway.

The ICC is 100% owned and controlled by Sun Hung Kai Properties (hereafter simply 'Sun Hung Kai'), whereas Two IFC is a fifty-fifty joint venture between Sun Hung Kai and the Henderson Land Group.

The heights of these two buildings were chosen to show due regard to their respective mountain backdrops. The ICC stands below Lion Rock (495 metres high) in what forms part of the distant Kowloon Foothills, while Victoria Peak, 552 metres high, is close behind Two IFC. Both developments were designed by globally renowned American architect firms following international design competitions; Cesar Pelli & Associates won the Two IFC design along with the remainder of the IFC buildings, and Kohn Pedersen Fox Associates won the ICC.

The requirements for the towers were to externally project strength and integrity in the classic skyscraper tradition. Internally, large floor plates were specified in order to meet the requirements of the target tenants who were anticipated to be financial institutions requiring spacious, high ceilinged open-plan trading floors. Two IFC has 88 storeys above ground and six below, providing 185,805 square metres of floor space with an average floor area of

Figure 3.1: Twin Tower entry to Hong Kong. Photograph courtesy of Sun Hung Kai Properties.

Figure 3.2: Twin Towers view from the Peak. Photograph courtesy of Sun Hung Kai Properties.

around 2,500 square metres. ICC, by comparison, has 108 floors above ground and four below, providing around 274,000 square metres of floor space with an average floor area of around 3,400 square metres and clear headroom as high as 3.15 metres; it boasts one of the world's highest hotels, the Ritz-Carlton, which occupies floors 102 to 118.

Despite the common practice of owners naming the buildings after its most important tenants, the two owners here decided not to allow the renaming of either building. However, due to the preponderance of banking and other financial institutions occupying the ICC (including three international investment banks), it quickly became known locally as the 'vertical Wall Street'. Two IFC's principal occupier is the Hong Kong Monetary Authority, which acquired fourteen high floors in 2001.

These two developments, both situated above the key Mass Transit Railway Corporation (MTR) Airport Railway stations that provide city check-ins to the airport, are excellent examples of the concept of 'Transit-Oriented Developments' (TOD). These can be described as intense urban developments within easy walking distance to major public transport nodes that benefit the people who work or live there. Sun Hung Kai started adopting this concept with New Town Plaza in Sha Tin (discussed in Chapter 5), along with YOHO Town in Yuen Long and Wings in Tseung Kwan O. They have become specialists in this form of development.

Placemaking

These two buildings have had a significant impact on placemaking on both the vertical and horizontal plane. In Cesar Pelli's own words, 'The Two IFC tower was designed to create a new gateway to the city and strike a simple, strong, and memorable presence – an obelisk at the scale of the city and the harbour.' Subsequent architectural commentaries have endorsed these words with observations such as 'It's a design that emphasises the buildings verticality, while endowing it with a sober sense of purpose and its obelisk form tapers with subtle setbacks which evoke a sense of ascension' (Singh 2019).

Paul Katz, the then president and managing principal of Kohn Pedersen Fox Associates, made the following remarks in 2011 on completion of the ICC building: 'One of the most important things about a tall building is its longevity. You design a building that you think is going to be there at least 100 or 150 years.' Writing in the *Architectural Record* in 2012 the editor commented on the completion of ICC that 'its quiet comportment serves as a welcome antidote to the hurly-burly of most Hong Kong high-rises.'

So, a century from now, what will the two sentinels of Victoria Harbour say about Hong Kong?

One of the key components to placemaking is pedestrian connectivity on the horizontal plane and in the urban context. Two IFC not only connects to the immediately adjoining IFC Mall, Four Seasons Hotel, and Four Seasons Place serviced apartments, but also reaches

Figure 3.3: Elevated footpath to Two IFC. Photograph courtesy of Sun Hung Kai Properties.

further towards the Central-Mid-Levels escalator, MTR stations, bus termini, outlying ferry piers, taxi stands, and the waterfront promenade. It also has a strong link with the Central Walkway System discussed in Chapter 1. Put together, it can be seen that the IFC gives local people another way to access and enjoy the harbour through scenic walks between work, retail, and dining destinations. Because of its close proximity to the Central Walkway System, it is clear that at the human public pedestrian level IFC enjoys a high degree of connectivity, with observers commenting that 'with cinemas, shops, restaurants with outdoor harbour view space, a gymnasium, and with ample provision of carparks, the IFC mall quickly became a place for people within and areas afar' (Singh 2019).

The relative isolation of Union Square (also known as Civic Square), in which the ICC is placed, is reflected by its comparatively poor public pedestrian access. This issue will be addressed in the design of the development atop the High-Speed Rail West Kowloon Station which, together with adjacent landscape decks and open space, will form a 1.5-kilometre-long pedestrian West Kowloon Parkway and link up with the existing residential populations in the hinterland of West Kowloon. The topside development is scheduled for completion between 2025 and 2026.

Figure 3.4: The West Kowloon Parkway. Photograph courtesy of Sun Hung Kai Properties.

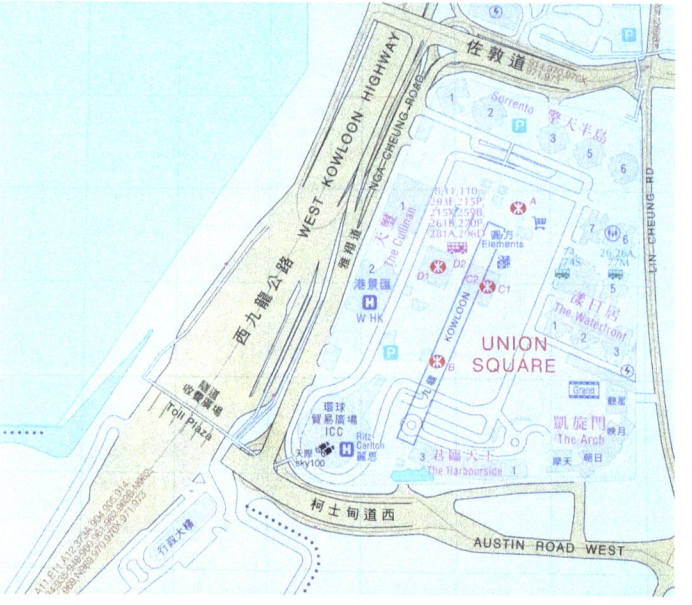

Figure 3.5: Union (Civic) Square – top-down map with transport links. Map courtesy of Sun Hung Kai Properties.

Figure 3.6: Sky100 – ICC Observation Deck. Photograph courtesy of Sun Hung Kai Properties.

The ICC is situated at the nexus of the High Speed Rail terminus, the Airport Railway, the Western Harbour Crossing, and the West Kowloon Cultural District. The design of the ICC allows (on payment) public access to the top floors of Hong Kong's highest indoor observation deck, sky100, and the Ritz-Carlton Hotel, both of which offer spectacular, unparalleled, 360-degree views. The West Kowloon Cultural District is still developing, but on completion, its dynamic art and cultural programmes will give a particular diversity to this area.

The Evolution of ICC's Master Planning

Sun Hung Kai won the tender for Kowloon Station development packages five, six, and seven in October 2000. Package five originally comprised two commercial buildings right in the middle of Union Square, as the above station development is known. In 2001 Sun Hung Kai successfully sought the Town Planning Board's approval to amend the Master Layout Plan to allow a reshuffling of the commercial gross floor area from the site of package five to both packages six and seven with higher buildings on both these sites. The ICC sits on the site of package seven. The minutes of the Town Planning Board (2001) meeting were very matter-of-fact in observing that 'the proposed deletion of two centrally located towers would

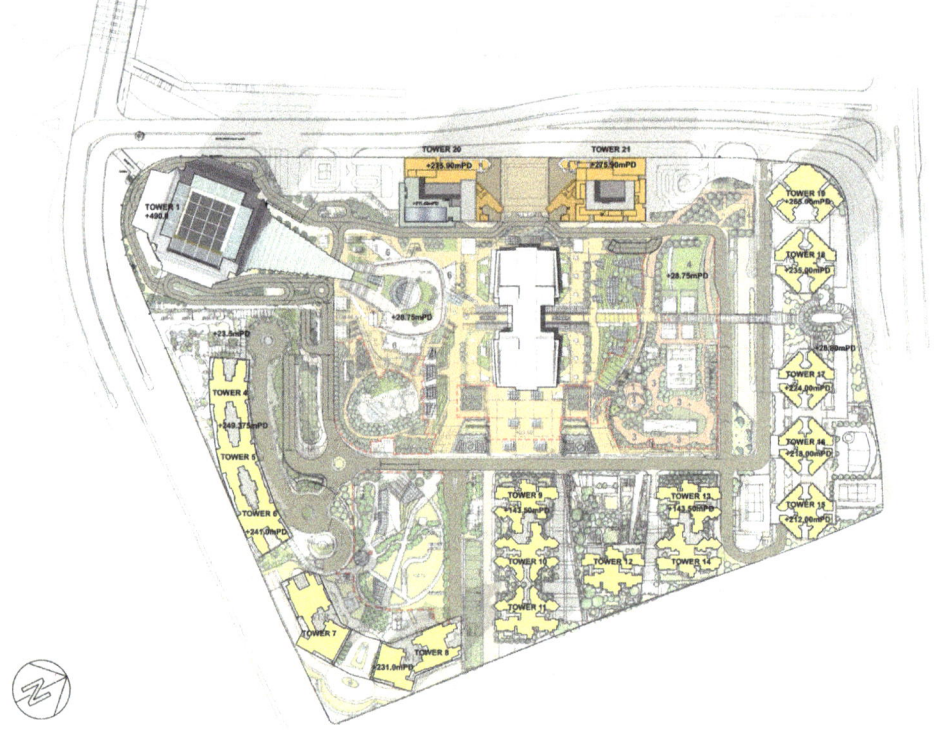

Figure 3.7: Union (Civic) Square – aerial view MLP. Photograph courtesy of Sun Hung Kai Properties.

result in better visual and physical permeability with a more open central plaza, recognising that the proposed development would be one of the tallest buildings in Southeast Asia.' It is only now, with the benefit of hindsight, that it can be seen that this decision had a positive effect on the placemaking of this development as demonstrated by the aerial view above of the completed master planning.

Union Square occupies a total area of 13.54 hectares, with a gross floor area of 1,090,026 square metres, approximately the same size as Canary Wharf in London. Because of its relative isolation it has been developed into a genuine, self-contained, mixed-use area with close to 6,000 residential units, 2,230 hotel rooms, and 2,490 serviced apartments, as well as the huge shopping mall Elements. Initially there were some sceptical property analysts who questioned whether or not the site was too remote for such a large-scale office development to be successful. Fortunately, however, they were proven wrong with Sun Hung Kai taking a longer term view of these sites' potential.

Prior to the starting of the construction work, Sun Hung Kai carried out various environmental and visual impact assessments as well as air ventilation assessments to ensure that their positive piece of placemaking would be successful. As a result, 400,000 square feet (approximately 37,160 square metres) of landscaped open space were created, with the undeveloped package five site allowing for a forecourt with alfresco dining areas for restaurant patrons and a breezeway generated in between the cluster of this mixed-use development. In addition, it allows the public, local residents, office workers, and hotel guests to enjoy an escalated promenade with a full view across to Hong Kong Island.

The placemaking approach was further enhanced through connectivity between the MTRC platforms and the shopping mall Elements, both with access up to the forecourt where the open space is largely used by the local resident and office community.

Recognising that good connectivity equates to good placemaking, connections will be further strengthened when the development atop the High Speed Rail West Kowloon Station – another TOD to be developed by Sun Hung Kai – comes into being.

Following on from the pattern set by the master plan of the ICC, the revised scheme (approved by the Town Planning Board in August 2021) features two sets of twin commercial towers with almost 100,000 square feet (roughly 9,300 square metres) of landscaped open space to be created at the podium level. Together with the 1.5-kilometre long West Kowloon Parkway, it will interconnect the surrounding residential neighbourhoods to the north with the pedestrian bridge network around Artist Square Tower to the west and south. Combined, this will give good public access not only to ICC and Union Square but also all the varied facilities in the West Kowloon Cultural District and the attractive West Kowloon Waterfront. It is envisaged that this enhanced connectivity will encourage newcomers and existing residents to create bonds with each other by way of their mutual enjoyment of these landscaped open spaces where community activities and events can be organized. In the past, the Union Square developments have been criticised for being disconnected from their surroundings, particularly for pedestrians. These planned arrangements should help mitigate this when they are completed. This greater connectivity has encouraged Sun Hung Kai to increase the retail component of this new scheme to provide better support for the greater footfall anticipated. Hence, this form of placemaking demonstrates a classic win-win situation for all the stakeholders, the public, tenants, and the landlord. (Figure 3.4 above shows how the West Kowloon Parkway will combine with the route via the Artist Square Towers to the harbour front.)

Construction Considerations

The ICC and Two IFC sites shared similar characteristics: being on newly created reclaimed land and their developers having to work around an existing station box. The constraints of having limited access and structures such as vent shafts to work around made mobility more difficult around the site, lengthening the construction period. The lessons taught by these challenges, particularly when designing the foundations and the building of Two IFC itself, were able to be carried forward to the design and construction of the ICC.

For example, in order to stiffen both buildings against the strong winds of the summer typhoon season, their respective structures were strengthened by four sets of outrigger systems at a separating interval of about twenty-five storeys. These systems allow for up to 300 millimetres lateral movement, which is considered to be well within the range for physical comfort. Both Two IFC and the ICC demonstrated their resilience during Typhoon Mangkhut in September 2018, Hong Kong's most intense storm on record, when the buildings sustained minimal damage despite their height in comparison to the extensive chaos that this super typhoon wreaked elsewhere in the city.

For the ICC, a unique construction challenge arose when the tenants Morgan Stanley decided to build and complete for occupation their lower sixteen office floors whilst at the same time allowing the construction of the upper floors to continue. It was necessary to provide a segregated construction access and a proper sense of entry for the Morgan Stanley zone while simultaneously providing access for workers and materials to complete the upper zones of the development. This was solved by an independent external access tower that gave vertical access for both the workers and their materials. There was fire and acoustic separation to ensure proper segregation for the two different parties, as well as other necessary measures to ensure site safety.

Efficient vertical circulation is critical to both buildings in order to cope with the high concentration of occupants, particularly at lunch time. Currently the ICC has a population of around 10,000 people. Double deck systems were installed with digitized on-demand lifts limited to distinct zones in order to maximize users and minimize circulation load.

Architectural Considerations

The architectural designers at Kohn Pedersen Fox Associates were very conscious of the ICC's status as a landmark. Its glass curtain wall is more reflective than that of Two IFC and the building is positioned in such a way that it reflects the afternoon light, turning the tower into a gleaming white column.

A shingle-style façade, resembling the scales of a dragon, articulates the subtle curvature along the vertical portion of the tower and is amplified at the base, creating canopies which protect occupants from downwind drafts along the hybrid curtain wall. The north facade features a dramatic entry point that has been coined the 'Dragon's Tail', flowing from the vertical plane and stretching along the horizontal plane towards the station plaza. The architects, in preparing their design, were fully aware that Kowloon means 'nine dragons' when translated into English.

The silver coated, low-E high performance glass shingles, as well as a system of sensors and monitors for heating, ventilation, and air conditioning, were developed with the Hong Kong Polytechnic University with the aim of reducing energy consumption by 15% compared with an average office building.

Figure 3.8: The Dragons Tail of ICC. Photograph courtesy of Sun Hung Kai Properties.

On completion, the ICC was awarded Hong Kong's first Platinum BEAM (Building Environmental Assessment Method) certification by the Hong Kong Green Building Council (HKGBC), a body that gives an independent assessment of the building's sustainability performance. Obtaining this certification was a requirement many international tenants had before the respective leases were signed, given that they demanded a very high standard of building for their staff to occupy.

Joseph Giovannini, a New York-based architect, critic, and author on architecture and design, elegantly and powerfully summed it all up as follows: 'The power of the building, then, resides in the design's inseparable relationship between the engineering and architecture. The engineering was determinant, but the design was transformative. Each grew from the other in this 118-storey intersection of art and technology. Each gave the other value' (Giovannini 2019, 204–8).

ICC's Development Timetable

- November 2005: Ground-breaking ceremony
- August 2007: Morgan Stanley confirmed to lease sixteen floors for their Hong Kong-based Asia Pacific headquarters
- December 2007: Credit Suisse enter into a long-term tenancy to occupy eleven floors
- December 2007: The ICC obtains a Temporary Occupation Permit for the lower sixteen floors
- May 2008: Deutsche Bank select twelve floors of ICC
- May 2008: Morgan Stanley move into their sixteen floors
- March 2010: The ICC obtains a full Occupation Permit

- April 2011: Opening of sky100 Observation Deck
- May 2011: The grand opening of Ritz-Carlton Hotel

ICC: One Decade On

In September 2020 the ICC achieved the 'Outstanding' rating, which was the highest honour under BREEAM In-Use, a green building assessment method by the British Research Establishment (BRE). The ICC obtained full marks in three assessment categories and became the first building in Hong Kong to be certified by BREEAM, putting it in the top 3% of green buildings around the globe.

It is a testament to the ICC's green management standards and its commitment to sustainable management that it is able to meet the expectations of its environmentally conscious tenants. From 2012 to 2022, through various energy saving measures, the ICC has conserved 20 million kilowatt-hours of energy, equivalent to the total annual electricity consumption of more than 6,000 three-member households and a reduction of 14,000 tonnes of carbon emissions.

In the same vein, the Council on Tall Buildings and Urban Habitats gave the ICC a 10-Year Award of Excellence in 2020, recognizing the proven value and performance of this tall building over a period of time. This award gives an opportunity to reflect back on tall buildings, such as the ICC, that have been completed and operational for a decade and acknowledge those projects that have performed successfully long after the ribbon-cutting ceremonies have passed.

Prior to these two awards, the HKGBC awarded ICC their Beam Plus Existing version certificate in October 2017, a first in Hong Kong. Put together, these three awards recognise the placekeeping efforts of Sun Hung Kai to maintain and enhance the initial high standard of their development.

Conclusion

In terms of placemaking and placekeeping, these two buildings play multiple roles: they remain the two highest buildings in Hong Kong, and at the macro level the twin obelisks serve as the dramatic and imposing gateway harbour entrance to Hong Kong. But they also have a very important role and impact at their respective local levels – they draw thousands of different people into them on a daily basis to work, shop, eat, sightsee, or travel using the many different modes of transport available at each site.

As discussed in this chapter, the IFC currently enjoys a much higher degree of public pedestrian connectivity when compared with the ICC. However, when the plans that are now in place are completed, the ICC's connectivity will be significantly enhanced as both the

West Kowloon Parkway and the pedestrian bridge network associated with the Artist Square Towers development will represent an important upgrade. This, in the Hong Kong context, is a key component to good placemaking.

Acknowledgements

I am most grateful to the positive support given to the writing of this chapter by Mr Raymond Kwok Ping-luen, chairman and managing director of Sun Hung Kai, and many members of the company who helped to ensure the accuracy of the text and provision of the visuals.

References

Giovannini, Joseph. 2019. 'Sentinal of Light.' In *The New Heart of Hong Kong: International Commerce Centre*, edited by Rebecca Lo. Oro Editions.

Lo, Rebecca. 2019. *The New Heart of Hong Kong: International Commerce Centre*. Oro Editions.

Singh, Amritpal. 2019. 'International Finance Centre / Cesar Pelli & Associates / Hong Kong.' *Civil, Architecture & Construction*, 30 March 2019. https://civilarchitectureconstruction.blogspot.com/2019/03/international-finance-centre-cesar.html.

Town Planning Board. 2001. 'Minutes of the 224th Metro Planning Committee.' 2 November 2001.

Twin Tower Gateway Entry into Victoria Harbour: Commentary (NC)

The western gateway to Victoria Harbour is now picturesquely defined by the gleaming twin towers of the ICC on the Kowloon side (built 2010) and Two IFC on Hong Kong Island (built 2003). At 484 metres and 412 metres tall, respectively, the ICC and Two IFC are the two tallest towers in Hong Kong and rank thirteenth and thirty-seventh among the tallest buildings in the world (Council on Tall Buildings and Urban Habitat 2025).

Taken together, can the ICC and Two IFC be seen not only as iconic structures, but also as iconic places in the city at multiple scales ranging from urban landmarks to public open spaces in private developments?

In other words, do large-scale developments such as these begin to redefine and expand the definition of 'placemaking' – beyond Jacobs' and Whyte's context of predominantly low-rise American and European urban developments – to consider the expansive scale of vertical urbanism in Hong Kong and other high-density Asian cities?

In contrast to comparably scaled urban developments in other world-leading cities, whether New York and Los Angeles in the US, London and Paris in Europe, Beijing and Shanghai in China, and others, the relationship of building to street in Hong Kong is typically more complex and interconnected in vertical stacking, mixing of functions, and circulation linkages at multiple levels to the city including its transport networks.

Figure 3.9: Union (Civic) Square – landscaped open space at ICC. Photograph courtesy of Sun Hung Kai Properties.

Figure 3.10: IFC – outdoor seating with harbour view. Photograph courtesy of Nelson Chen.

In *Cities Without Ground*, Hong Kong is studied and mapped as a city without a singularly defined ground plane due to its complex three-dimensional massing, connectivity, and scale (Frampton, Solomon, and Wong 2012). (Note: some case studies have been discussed in earlier chapters of this book, such as the elevated footbridges of Central and public spaces at ground and elevated within private developments at Taikoo Place and Taikoo Shing.)

Both the ICC and Two IFC are high-rise commercial and transit-oriented developments with retail podiums atop a multi-transit hub of underground rail system, ground level bus terminals, and public transport interchanges. The ICC and Elements shopping mall are situated above the high-speed rail to China, whereas Two IFC has linked access via covered footbridges to ferry services for crossing the harbour and the outlying islands.

In both examples, public access to retail malls and office lobbies are made at multiple levels other than street level. The traditional streetscapes of typical American and European cities are not present in these two mega-scale developments, which are actually 'islands' surrounded by multi-lane roads. Shopping arcades and elevated footbridges above become the de facto 'street' experience. Public spaces include outdoor plazas and indoor atriums, as well as more expansive public concourses and gardens on podium roofs which are not easy to find but, once discovered, offer quiet oases amidst the intense urban activity below.

In both instances, public open spaces have been designed within private developments, demonstrating the commitment by their commercial developers and property managers to placemaking as well as placekeeping. At the ICC, the roof podium garden connects the entire residential complex as well as the aforementioned retail mall and high-speed trains to China situated below. At one end, Union Square is surrounded by restaurants with outdoor dining near the base of the ICC tower. Across the harbour, Two IFC has a much smaller, publicly accessible roof podium, but provides pockets of landscaped terrace seating overlooking the harbour.

As vertical cities within the city, both the ICC and Two IFC developments demonstrate multiple scales of placemaking in the context of high-density vertical urbanism.

Key Notes

1. Placemaking in the context of high-density vertical urbanism.
2. Placemaking at multiple scales from macro to micro.
3. Public outdoor space in private developments.

References

Council on Tall Buildings and Urban Habitat. 2023. 'Tallest Buildings.' https://www.skyscrapercenter.com/buildings/.

Frampton, Adam, Jonathan D. Solomon, and Clara Wong. 2012. *Cities Without Ground: A Hong Kong Guidebook*. Oro Editions.

4
Lai Chi Wo: Exemplar of Sustainable Cultural Heritage Conservation

The Story, So Far

In December 2020, it was announced that the Lai Chi Wo (LCW) project had received Special Recognition for Sustainable Development under the 2020 UNESCO Asia-Pacific Awards for Cultural Heritage Conservation. The UNESCO Jury applauded the project's pioneering approach to rural sustainability that 'transforms notions of heritage practice from its conventional focus on material conservation to encompass living heritage in all its manifestations . . . the project demonstrates the importance of interweaving nature and cultural heritage in setting a new urban-rural sustainability agenda for the Hong Kong SAR and beyond.'

The receipt of this international award and recognition represents the culmination of eight years' hard work led by the Policy for Sustainability Lab under the Centre for Civic Society and Governance at the University of Hong Kong (HKU). This was done in close collaboration with the Hong Kong Countryside Foundation (HKCF), Conservancy Association, Produce Green Foundation, as well as a wide cross-section of dedicated individuals, professionals, stakeholders, and crucially, the villagers themselves, who all shared a common interest and goal of achieving a sustainable rural development solution for this unique village.

To give some historical context of LCW, the following information has been extracted from the Statement of Historical and Cultural Significance prepared by Professor Lau Chi-pang of the Department of History at Lingnan University to accompany the HKCF's Town Planning Board submission made in late 2018.

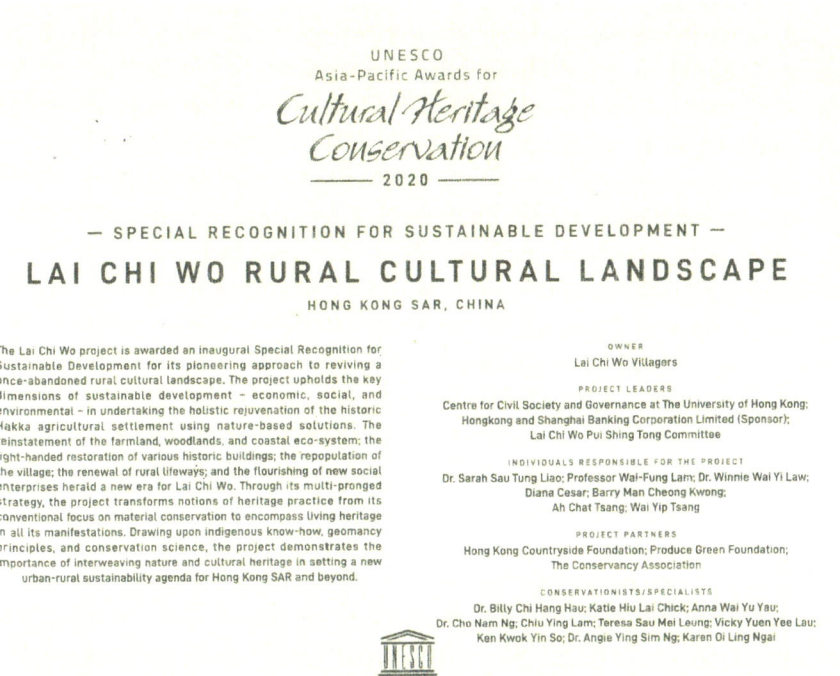

Figure 4.1: UNESCO Asia-Pacific Award for Cultural Heritage Conservation – 2020. Photograph courtesy of UNESCO.

The village was established about 400 years ago by two Hakka clans – the Wongs and the Tsangs – from mainland China. It became the largest self-sustaining Hakka walled village in the north-eastern New Territories that relied principally on farming, fishing, and wood cutting. Its highest population is claimed to have been about 1,000 in the late 1960s and early 1970s before most of the villagers moved away (many to the United Kingdom and Europe) for their livelihood.

The village layout follows the typical Hakka style with about 220 houses of various types formed in three vertical lanes and nine horizontal rows with a central axis, protected by *feng shui* woodlands and hills at the back and guarded by walls, gates, and watercourse at the front. Most of the existing buildings are between forty and one hundred years old, many having been rebuilt in the 1960s and 70s. They mostly retain traditional Hakka house architectural character defining elements including tiled roofs, brick, stone, and rammed earth walls, brick cooking stoves, and chimneys.

The built heritage of the village is an important cultural asset as it represents the historical layers of the local built environment in places with traditional vernacular Hakka architecture and construction. Together, they demonstrate the cultural, social, educational,

Figure 4.2: Hip Tin Temple and Hok Shan Monastery. Photograph courtesy of The Hong Kong Countryside Foundation (HKCF).

environmental, and religious values of LCW. The Hip Tin Temple and Hok Shan Monastery are good examples with both being listed as Grade 3 historic buildings by the Antiquities and Monuments Office. The temple is thought to have been built in 1900 as indicated by its wall paintings.

The Agricultural Revitalization Programmes

The HKCF was established in 2011 to enable people keen to conserve the countryside for the long-term benefit of the Hong Kong public to jointly make dreams come true by implementing practical local action plans step by step. This particular story was started by two of the directors of HKCF, the late Dr Cho-Nam Ng and Chiu Ying Lam, who had already identified LCW as a potential and suitable target for transformation from a de-populated village into a vibrant farming village with a residential population. By this time, the 400-year-old historical village was abandoned and overgrown with many of the original houses crumbling into dilapidation. If nothing was done, the village would be consigned to oblivion and Hong Kong would never get to understand the historical circumstances that brought the early settlers here in line with their wisdom of 'living near hills, seek nourishment from the hills; living by the seaside, seek nourishment from the sea.' In other words, their way of getting daily necessities from nature without damaging its harmony was an achievement that we today call 'sustainable development'.

During their early visits in 2009, Lam and Ng got to meet important local village leaders including Yuk-On Tsang, who was now retired and who shared the same interest in promoting village revival.

They agreed that the remoteness of LCW, being only accessible by foot or sea, meant it had not caught the attention of property developers or other outsiders and would therefore be able to retain its original natural beauty and authenticity with this geographical advantage.

In those early days Lam also met, by chance, David Tsang (David) who was a villager who had gone abroad as a teenager. After several decades of life overseas he wished to return and settle down, but found the village deserted. He had forgotten the farming techniques he had learned as a child, but he dreamt that by the time he passed away LCW could be restored to one third of its former beauty when he was young. This story reminded Lam and Ng that now was the best time to take action to revitalize the village. They realized that the villagers like David who had left during the 1960s and 1970s had also reached retirement age, had also retained their strong affection for the village, and shared the same dream for its restoration. Any delay would result in the buildings and the fields being degraded beyond recovery. It was against this background that the HKCF came into being.

Effectively starting from scratch, the HKCF had no idea how to go about agricultural or village revitalization but understood that farming was the basis of Hakka culture and being in harmony with nature was the acquired wisdom of Hakka villagers, with their architectural cluster being the tangible feature of villages such as LCW. Multiple site visits were organized for various scholars, experts, non-government organizations, and volunteers. Subjects covered included agriculture, architecture, history, geography, culture, ecology, education, planning, and sustainable development. The purpose of these visits was to gradually promote the concept of LCW revitalization to society and at the same time, through interdisciplinary exchanges, try to understand from the many and varied perspectives what the issues that needed to be considered and taken care of were in preparing the revitalization plan.

In parallel with these site visits, the HKCF, building on the good relationship already established with Yuk-On and David, organized meetings to expand contacts with more of the villagers, hoping this would progressively build up communication and mutual trust with many more of them. Crucially, a good relationship was subsequently nurtured with the two village representatives, Wai-Yip Tsang and Ah-Chat Tsang, who were convinced that the HKCF were genuinely sincere in their efforts to build a future for the village without having any hidden vested interest.

By 2012, HKCF started to think about possible models of village revitalization and organized a seminar in which speakers talked about similar village programmes abroad.

Surprisingly, around 40 people attended, including the two village heads and several other elders who came all the way into town to listen to the talks. This was seen as a very positive and encouraging development.

The next major step forward occurred in 2013 when the Hongkong Bank Foundation (the philanthropic arm of HSBC) decided to support the 'Sustainable Lai Chi Wo Programme' at HKU and kickstart the revitalization of LCW with the formation of an interdisciplinary and multi-organizational team.

The Programme aimed at rejuvenating LCW village and developing a viable model for rural revitalization grounded upon a sustainable approach. To achieve this goal, the Programme worked on agricultural rehabilitation, community revitalization, education, and research with a focus on forging social innovation and cross-sectoral collaboration, while all the time working closely with the villagers of LCW (Law 2018).

The resumption of farming constituted the starting point of the revitalization and was complemented by a range of diversified activities. The Programme sought to bring life back to LCW and to wake the farming village that had lain dormant for three to four decades. As one of the partnering organizations, the HKCF had a major role to play communicating with the villagers to encourage their support and participation in the Programme, in particular by leasing their fields for farming rehabilitation which would be fundamental in order to underpin the whole project.

Initially, around five hectares of farmland were identified for the Programme, but the problems of absentee and fragmented ownership together with poorly kept land records were immediate obstacles that needed to be tackled and overcome. How could the HKCF identify and reach the many landowners to discuss the leasing of their land?

Fortunately, the local connections that had already been established proved useful and David, the original lone indigenous villager who was the first to come back to till his land, proposed a unique 'ABC model' where 'A' referred to the landowners of LCW, 'B' referred to an intermediary company recognized and trusted by the villagers, and 'C' referred to the HKCF. Landowners could lease their lands to the trusted intermediary and the HKCF would only need to sign one lease agreement with the intermediary as a means to rent the farmland desired. This ABC model provided a pragmatic solution to the trust issue because the intermediary could facilitate the conclusion of the individual farmland leases despite the HKCF having not yet secured the trust of all the landowners.

With the support of the village chiefs, David reached out to fellow villagers both in Hong Kong and those residing overseas. This needed a strong and determined effort on his part requiring many phone calls, WhatsApp, WeChat, and email messages and communications. He even flew to the UK to persuade those who were unsure of or sceptical about the Programme. His highly committed endeavours enabled the HKCF to sign the lease agreement for about 3.8 hectares or 410,337 square feet of land on 23 October 2013, a date that became the official starting date of the farm rehabilitation Programme. The first 6-year term has now concluded and a further 6-year term, up until 2025, has been agreed upon and signed. The new agreement included an expansion of the area to around 467,000 square feet (4.3 hectares), as some new lots were added due to more landowners including their land in the project. This is another good sign of the advancing mutual trust between the parties.

In the new 6-year lease, 'B' has been replaced by the Lai Chi Wo Pui Shing Tong Committee, a society registered under the Societies Ordinance and recognized by both UNESCO and in the American Institute of Architects awards to properly represent the interests of the village owners. The establishment of this committee, which comprises representatives of both the Tsang and Wong clans and various family branches of the village, was an important step towards the engagement of all the indigenous villagers, whether at home or abroad, in a wider more structured way. The committee further represents a move away from the previous more traditional autocratic form of governance and the introduction of modern concepts of community development and village management.

Here is a timeline showing examples of some subsequent events and activities that took place. The events demonstrate how the project evolved as a result of the collaboration between the various organizations, stakeholders, and villagers:

2014

After the Produce Green Foundation had taken the lead in opening up the initial farming area for recultivation, the first rice crop was harvested in July. The same year, at the time of the Chung Yeung Festival, home grown rice was served to the overseas villagers who had returned to pay their respects to their ancestors. This was hugely symbolic as a clear sign that the revitalization had begun and stimulated a lot of interest in the overseas visitors.

This year saw the start of what has now become an annual village cleaning event, mobilized by the project team and the new LCW community working together with HKU, the Conservancy Association, and the villagers.

2015

(i) A draft Outline Zoning Plan was gazetted for the area that showed significant areas of traditional farming land; this area was zoned as both 'Conservation Area' and 'Green Belt'. On behalf of both the villagers and the Programme, the HKCF submitted an objection to the plan and with Ng attending, the Town Planning Board meeting was able to persuade the Board to rezone these lands back to agricultural use. This was well received by the villagers and helped demonstrate the HKCF's ongoing commitment to the project. The Lai Chi Wo, Siu Tan and Sam A Tsuen Outline Zoning Plan No. S/NE-LCW/2, gazetted on 19 February 2016, duly reflected these changes and at the same time confirmed that the village itself had been identified as a 'Cultural Hub'.

(ii) Up until this time, the only sea access was via charter boats from Sha Tau Kok, which necessitated obtaining Closed Area Permits for non-residents to get to LCW. As more and more outsiders were getting involved, this was proving an obstacle to progress. Lam and Ng were able to advise Yuk An Tsang, Chairman of the Sha Tau Kok Rural Committee on the matter. As a result, starting in January 2016, there was a regular Sunday kaito service from Ma Liu Shui to LCW and back for the convenience of everyone.

(iii) One of the effects of this new ferry service has been a significant increase in the number of visitors and tourists coming to the village, which helped to enhance economic activity and publicity for ongoing work.

(iv) To meet growing demand, a trial twice mid-week ferry service began operation in July 2022, initially subsidized by the Countryside Conservation Office (CCO). It is now operating as a viable service.

2016

Ng invited a China Light and Power (CLP) senior management team to visit LCW on a particularly cold January day. Following this visit, CLP committed to simultaneously upgrading power supply to LCW and reconnecting power to neighbouring Mui Tsz Lam and Kop Tong villages. Naturally, these improvements were very well received by the villagers and have helped stimulate some modest revitalization works at those two other villages.

In 2016, Lonely Planet's Best in Asia index ranked Hong Kong among the top ten Asian destinations; it highlighted the revitalizing LCW as one of the 'must see' sites to visit.

2017

(i) The 'Three Dous' Community Farming Incubation Scheme was added to the HKU's research-based farm, which sought to provide training and assistance to indigenous villagers and individuals who aspired to join the revitalization work. The scheme would prepare them to develop community-based agricultural production. 'Dou' is a traditional agricultural unit related to rice farming and is equivalent to 7,260 square feet (674 square metres) of land. The name 'Three Dous' is used to describe small farms. Initially, seven such small-scale community farms were established; this number was then expanded to nine. Their produce and products were promoted online and sold at the monthly Lai Chi Wo Farmers' Market. The market had been started earlier in the year by the Policy for Sustainability Lab, demonstrating that a thriving agricultural community was taking shape and could possibly serve as a model for other village revitalization projects to follow.

(ii) The Sustainable Lai Chi Wo Programme was successfully completed in September 2017. Building on this solid foundation, the Policy for Sustainability Lab received further support from Hongkong Bank Foundation to continue its work at LCW. The new Programme – 'HSBC Rural Sustainability' – ran from October 2017 through to September

Figure 4.3: Lai Chi Wo Market. Photograph courtesy of HKCF.

2022. It is focused on scaling up the revitalization effort through creating more partnerships, incubating socio-economic models, and developing strategies. In order to achieve this objective, the Policy for Sustainability Lab established the Academy for Sustainable Communities under the Centre for Civil Society and Governance, so as to promote rural sustainability not only in LCW but also to create a model that could be applied to other villages in the New Territories (Policy for Sustainability Lab 2018–2021).

(iii) Partnering with the Conservancy Association, the HKCF was successful in obtaining funding from the government's Environmental and Conservation Fund to continue and expand the work set out in the 'Management Agreement Scheme at Lai Chi Wo Enclave'. A budget of HK$7 million was allocated for 2017–19 and HK$8 million for 2019–21. The following are some examples of the activities that were organized: in 2018 they co-organised a LCW Harvest Fun Fair under the Management Agreement, and again in 2019 a Summer Fun Fair was held. In November 2022, the Harvest Fun Fair was successfully revived after a hiatus of 3 years.

2018

The Academy for Sustainable Communities launched a 'Certificate in Sustainable Communities' programme, whose curriculum consists of four modules: Understanding Cultural Landscape (which UNESCO helpfully defines as the 'combined works of nature and man that express a diversity of manifestations of the interactions between humankind and the natural environment'), Sustainable Agriculture, Introduction to Local Ecology, and Community Partnerships.

The course includes seminars, forums, and field-based activities, with the LCW Field Leader Training module being particularly popular.

2019

The Academy for Sustainable Communities Community Partnership module was launched to introduce basic theoretical foundations and applied skills in building community-based urban-rural partnerships for sustainability to the wider Hong Kong population.

In December, the decennial Tai Ping Ching Chiu Festival of Sha Tau Kok Hing Chun Yeuk's seven villages, which includes LCW and has persisted for many generations, took place. Also known as the Da Chiu Festival, the four-day event took over a year to prepare with the participation of more than a thousand villagers. With past experiences and collective attachments, villagers went through all the dignified traditional rituals smoothly. Although many young villagers returned to join the festival, most of them reside overseas, and villagers who are the bearers of the festival are getting old. Festivals such as this one are a good example of 'intangible cultural heritage'. However, in order to conserve and safeguard this type of intangible cultural heritage, those involved cannot rely just on master-and-apprentice and intergenerational succession, but also require the concerted efforts of the government, businesses, academia, and other stakeholders in society to ensure their long-term sustainability and viability.

As suggested by UNESCO, this urban-rural symbiosis is the only viable way forward and needs to be continually nurtured in order to make revitalization of these rural areas sustainable in the long term. Put quite simply, these areas will not be able to survive without the presence of non-indigenous villagers. Through the work of the Policy for Sustainability Lab and their offspring, the Academy for Sustainable Communities, the greater public has awareness and education on the subject. As can be seen by the make-up of the community farm projects, the number of outsiders participating is now far greater than local villagers. This trend is surely the way forward. With the right training and education, the new settlers have been able to adapt and blend in with the indigenous community who, in turn, increasingly understand the importance of this inter-relationship in order for there to be a sustainable long-term solution to the survival of the village. Between October 2013 and September 2022, the Hongkong Bank Foundation funded the HKU-initiated Sustainable Lai Chi Wo

Figure 4.4: Da Chiu Festival – 2019. Photograph courtesy of HKCF.

Figure 4.5: Villagers celebrate the restoration of the East Gate – 2024. Photograph courtesy of HKCF.

Figure 4.6: Villagers celebrate the restoration of the East Gate – 2024. Photograph courtesy of HKCF.

and Rural Sustainability Programmes, which have engaged thousands of individual participants and is now beginning to reap rewards.

The following data provided by HKU as of November 2022 shows the progress that has been made so far.

When the first programme was launched in 2013, only one household lived in the village on a regular basis. As reported by HKU in November 2022, that number grew to nineteen households with a population of about thirty-six living in the village as regular residents, with seven from the indigenous community, eight new settlers, and four project-based employees.

There are currently nine community farm groups with around seventy-two members; twenty-three were from the indigenous community; twenty were new settlers, farmers, and volunteers; and twenty-nine were project workers.

These growing numbers help demonstrate the impact of the principal twin drivers behind these rehabilitation programmes. The HKCF did crucial work to win the trust of the villagers and led to them leasing their lands of sufficient area; this in turn provided the platform for HKU's programmes to grow and become established and subsequently be recognized by the UNESCO award.

Lai Chi Wo

Figure 4.7: Aerial photo – Lai Chi Wo Village and farmland. Photograph courtesy of HKCF.

One interesting experiment conducted by HKU was to investigate whether or not some of the rehabilitated farmland could be successfully planted with Arabica coffee trees. In the summer of 2021, they reported that around 700 trees had been planted; the first batch of coffee cherries were produced the previous year and, suitably dried, were processed to deliver a local shade-grown coffee. Lai Chi Wo coffee drip bags are now available for coffee lovers to try.

The HKCF and Conservancy Association then secured funding from the CCO to renew the Management Agreement for the three-year period 2021–2024. The intention is for this project to follow the framework of 'Nature-based Solutions', which are actions to protect, sustainably manage, or restore natural ecosystems.

The Village House Restoration programme

Under the Chief Executive's Community Project List 2016, the HKCF was granted a sum of nearly HK$50 million by the Hong Kong Jockey Club Charities Trust in August 2016 to conserve and renew a group of village houses as the operation base of experiential learning programmes and to provide accommodation for programme participants. The group of houses, known as 'Hakka Life Experience Village @Lai Chi Wo' (HLEV@LCW), will be operated as an integral entity with any profit being applied to the ongoing maintenance of the houses.

Two Section 16 Applications for thirty houses were made to the Town Planning Board to obtain the necessary approval for Hotel (Holiday House) Use. However, only fifteen houses gained this approval because of budgetary constraints and the higher-than-expected restoration costs caused by the specialized work and the remote location. The first approval was given in August 2017 and the second in February 2019. Serving as a pilot scheme, the house restoration contract for the first batch of two houses commenced in June 2018 and was completed in December 2019; the second batch restorations for four houses started in October 2019 and was completed in February 2021. Work on the third and final batch of nine houses started in December 2020 and was completed in time for the official opening ceremony on 17 December 2022.

These works have been able to proceed in spite of the fact that not all the villagers were supportive at the outset. They criticized the selection and choice of houses to be restored and the lack of an overall masterplan for the village restoration. In the end, work proceeded with the house owners who were prepared to participate. Hopefully, the completed houses will help persuade those who doubted the merits of the project to change their minds.

Where possible, the restoration work is being done carefully and sensitively using traditional materials and construction techniques in order to retain the existing character and integrity of both the houses and the village as a whole. It is hoped that the project will showcase an innovative approach to village revitalization that will conserve the architectural, cultural, natural, and scenic values through collaboration with local villagers and promote sustainable development in LCW.

A full range of pictures and images of the before and after situation of these restored houses can be viewed at https://lcwhakkalife.wixsite.com/hakkalifeprogram.

Each of the fifteen houses have been leased by the individual village owner(s) to the HKCF at a nominal rent for twenty years. The HKCF undertook to restore each house at an average capital work cost of around HK$2 million per house. On completion of the works, the owner can come and occupy his house for a nominated two-week period in each of the following years, usually for the celebration of traditional Chinese festivals such as the welcoming of the New Year, the Chung Yeung Festival, and the Ching Ming Festival. If the owner wishes to take back his house at the end of the first ten years, this can be done on reimbursement of 50% of the restoration costs and then on a sliding scale down towards the twentieth year, after which he can recover the house without any charge. These house owners appreciate keeping the traditional style of a single-storey Hakka house with a tiled roof, which preserves the integrity of the overall appearance and ensures a high conservation value for the village as a whole. Adopting this structure and approach demonstrates good collaboration between both parties that has encouraged the villagers to participate and, hopefully, to return and live

Figure 4.8: Before and After – House Restoration – 2022. Photograph courtesy of HKCF.

here. This could potentially prove to be a model for other villages to follow. However, it must be remembered that the LCW villagers are a rare, possibly unique, breed of indigenous New Territories villagers who thus far have eschewed taking advantage of the 'Small House' policy that has resulted in so many other villages being cluttered and spoiled by new unplanned building development (Nissim 2022). It will be hard to find another village whose landowners will agree to adopt a similar approach towards conservation.

The 'Holiday Flat' guesthouse licence application was submitted to the Office of Licensing Authority in November 2020. The requirements of statutory works regarding building safety and fire safety were received from the Office of Licensing Authority, and it took a year of negotiations, facilitated by the CCO, to find solutions to the rather onerous requirements demanded by the Fire Services Department.

Between 2017 and 2020, the HKCF successfully conducted twelve Experiential Learning programmes with 500 man-hours participation. The initial Experiential Learning package included thematic activity programmes and delivered training to villagers, potential guides and docents, and volunteers. The topics covered included guided tours, trails, workshops, events, exhibitions, publications, and more. This capacity-building component is seen as a critical element of the overall project that ensures that the invaluable assets residing in HLEV@LCW will be wisely used to help establish and run a viable, sustainable business model.

Countryside Conservation Office

The Hong Kong Chief Executive's 2017 Policy Address heralded more proactive government involvement in order to support the work of organizations such as the HKCF. The CCO was established under the Environmental Protection Department at the end July 2018 and has stated that it will prioritize helping to enhance countryside revitalization at LCW.

The CCO has been instrumental in facilitating communications with other departments, as this pioneering project was faced with a lot of statutory regulatory challenges. The challenges are mainly caused by the nature of certain legal requirements which were designed and written for an urban setting which, if applied to LCW's rural setting, would be impossible to comply with.

The CCO has its own funding scheme and in August 2020, the HKCF were advised that their applications for the following projects had been approved:

1. A feasibility study of licensing food businesses in remote villages
2. A review of traditional craftsmanship and cultural inheritance in LCW
3. A project to study the feasibility of enhancing ferry transportation via Tolo harbour to LCW and nearby villages for marine ecotourism
4. the 'Prevention of Deterioration of Built Environment and Landscape Improvement in Lai Chi Wo Village' project

Funding for the first two two-year programmes enabled them to start in early 2021. The HKCF partnered with the Hong Kong Historic Building Conservation Association for the second of these two programmes. The third program was approved and a trial mid-week service was started in July 2022.

These worthwhile projects had all ended by 30 June 2023.

The fourth project deserves particular mention. At the time of writing, there is no public sewer serving LCW, so the HKCF sought the CCO's agreement to provide a small sewage treatment works in the village as a long-term solution that would replace the existing septic tank and soakaway systems. Such an upgrade was well justified, given the close proximity of the village to both the Yan Chau Tong Marine Park and the ecologically important stream – not to mention the revitalized adjoining farmland! Funding of HK$1 billion was earmarked for the CCO, half of which was to be invested in such non-recurrent improvements to local infrastructure, so the negotiations will continue on what will be a very challenging project to both design and build.

In the meantime, for the renovated houses, septic tank and soakaway systems will be adopted with design and specification standards that satisfy or go beyond the guidelines set out in the Practice Note for Professional Persons (ProPECC Note PN 5/93) on Building (Standards of Sanitary Fitments, Plumbing, Drainage Works and Latrines) Regulations 40(1), 40 (2), 41(1) and 90. This will hopefully have eliminated impacts on the adjoining freshwater and marine environments by containing waste water and preventing direct discharge into surrounding habitats of high ecological value.

HakkaHome at LCW

The HakkaHome at LCW is a social enterprise that was formed by LCW indigenous villagers with the support of the HKCF and has acquired 'charitable institution' status and tax exemption under Section 88 of the Inland Revenue Ordinance. It applied for funds from the CCO to carry out a pilot scheme that would manage and improve the environmental and hygiene conditions of the village and recruit villagers as ambassadors to publicize the message of upkeeping the environmental hygiene of the village. The funds would also be used to remove the dangerous structures of some ruined buildings and landscape them to become community gardens. These activities would help further revitalize the village while ensuring the best environmental and cultural conservation practices are followed:

(a) To set up and run a sustainable business with a view to revitalizing the LCW Village, creating job opportunities for the villagers and at the same time preserving the integrity of the existing Hakka village houses, the culture, the beautiful rural environment, and the high ecological value of the area.

(b) To develop and promote LCW Village as an education hub on sustainable development in Hong Kong by introducing green and sustainable practices in its daily operation; delivering and facilitating a wide variety of cultural and training activities; and facilitating the building of eco infrastructure or adoption of green technologies, thus creating a win-win-win situation for the local community, the environment, and the Hong Kong society at large.

(c) To be an independent, self-governing, accountable, membership-based, charitable, and non-profit organization.

In September 2022, the 'Prevention of Deterioration of Built Environment and Landscape Improvement in Lai Chi Wo Village' project was launched with a 'Public Planting Day'. Three dilapidated house sites, with the agreement of the owners, were converted into medium-term landscaped open spaces for the use of the village community and visitors.

In addition to the fifteen houses being restored by the HKCF, HKU reported that as at November 2022, thirty-eight of the villagers have, on their own initiative and at their own cost, rehabilitated their own houses, with twenty of them being rented out. Again, this is positive proof that the village is slowly but surely coming back to life.

In 2018, the Survey and Mapping Office of the Lands Department issued Edition 8 of their Countryside Series of maps for the North East and Central New Territories. This edition included a guide map to the village with some of the highlights to be visited and enjoyed.

Figure 4.9: Survey Mapping Office – Lai Chi Wo – 2018. Photograph from Hong Kong Map Service 2.0, Lands Department.

At the beginning of this chapter, it was stated that the HKCF was established with the objective of working together with various stakeholders to try and make the LCW conservation dream come true. Villager David Tsang shared this dream; with all that has been achieved so far and all that is planned for the future, there is a very good chance – even though the overall project is still a work in progress – of that dream coming true.

Endorsements

An independent recognition of all the work that has been, and continues to be, done at LCW came in November 2021 when all the parties involved received the following citation from the American Institute of Architects Hong Kong Chapter 'for the ongoing collaborative efforts of individuals and organizations in heritage conservation of this historic Hakka walled settlement, including revitalization of its traditional farming and cultural landscapes together with a number of houses, thereby promoting sustainable rural community development and encouraging effective control over rural land use in the New Territories.'

The more recent endorsement and recognition was reported in September 2022. On 14 August 2022, the final round of the Sixth China Post-graduate Case Competition of Public Management was finished in Zhengzhou. Over 11,000 participants under 2,110 groups from 211 schools joined the competition. The winner was the team from the School of Public Policy and Management of Tsinghua University, who presented the case of village revitalization of LCW in Hong Kong.

That this team won the competition demonstrates how important the revitalization of rural villages in China has become; all the work that has been done in LCW could, potentially, be used as a reference model for the whole of China.

On 27 March 2023, the Hong Kong Institute of Architectural Conservationists (HKICON) informed the HKCF that the LCW project was the winner of the HKICON Conservation Awards 2022 under the Adaptive Reuse category. The following is an extract from their Jury Panel citation: 'The adaptive reuse of twelve vacant village houses in Lai Chi Wo gives new impetus to revitalization of Hong Kong's best preserved Hakka village. The appropriate new use as guesthouses is inserted in the historic fabric with innovative, minimal, and reversible interventions that also functionally upgrade the houses to meet modern-day requirements. The project demonstrates an individual approach to the village house typologies, where conservation techniques with interpretative story-telling methods reveal the spirit of the place. This initiative reflects – and relates to – the larger vision of a sustainable future for Lai Chi Wo and serves as an excellent example for conservation of rural heritage in Hong Kong.'

In the modern context, this project represents an excellent rural example of both place-making and placekeeping working together to find a long-term sustainable formula that ensures the viable and ongoing conservation of this unique village.

References

The Hong Kong Countryside Foundation. n.d. 'Hakka Life Experience Village @ Lai Chi Wo.' Accessed 20 March 2025. https://lcwhakkalife.wixsite.com/hakkalifeprogram.

Law, Winnie. 2018. *Vivifying Lai Chi Wo: Sustainable Lai Chi Wo Programme Four Year Review and Outlook*. Policy for Sustainability Lab.

Nissim, Roger. 2022. *Land Administration and Practice in Hong Kong*. Fifth edition. Hong Kong University Press.

Policy for Sustainability Lab. 2018–2021. *Rural Sustainability*. Half yearly editions, from Autumn 2018 to Summer 2021. Centre for Civil Society and Governance, The University of Hong Kong. www.socsc.hku.hk/psl.

Acknowledgements

I am extremely grateful to the Chairman of the HKCF Mr Lam Chiu Ying, former Project Director David Au, and Senior Project Manager Teresa Leung for all their help and encouragement in compiling this chapter, proofreading and correcting the text, and sourcing the pictures and images.

My thanks also to the HKU Centre for Civil Society and Governance for sharing all the data they have, over the years, collected about the village.

Lai Chi Wo Cultural Heritage Conservation: Commentary (NC)

LCW is a historic Hakka walled village in the northeast corner of the New Territories with origins dating back nearly four centuries. In recent years, with the support of several charities, university research centres and NGO conservancy groups, including the Centre for Civic Society and Governance of HKU and the HKCF, this abandoned village has been undergoing restorations as an ongoing sustainable revitalisation project.

In terms of placemaking, LCW offers a different approach than usually associated with the design of social spaces in densely populated urban areas, such as streetscapes and public parks. Instead of placemaking, the process of heritage conservation at LCW may be seen more as placekeeping or place restoration of a rural cultural landscape. Even so, it involves a similar approach and commitment to planning, designing, and managing quality places for people – in this case, not only return stays for the ancestral villagers but also rural retreats for ecocultural tours or countryside visits by urban residents.

Figure 4.10: Overhead view of Lai Chi Wo. Photograph courtesy of the Hong Kong Countryside Foundation.

As a reminder, over 75% of the land area of Hong Kong is unbuilt, and the majority of this open space is set aside for country parks. LCW lies near the Plover Cove Country Park as well as the Yan Chau Tong Marine Park. With its resurrected farming activity under an agricultural revitalisation programme and its traditional buildings renovated under a village house restoration programme, this Hakka-style village is being re-energised as a place layered with cultural, social, and environmental heritage that inspires its visiting public as well as gives house owners of the founding village clans a reason to return.

In this connection, it is important to highlight the leading role of NGOs as champions for rural placemaking, much as property developers are often the leading influencers in urban planning and development. At LCW, it takes literally a village of different stakeholders to save this village by restoring and revitalising its physical and cultural heritage (Centre for Civil Society and Governance, The University of Hong Kong, n.d.).

Thus, rural placemaking and cultural landscapes play significant roles in the conservation and restoration of historical sites amidst the natural habitats that surround densely urbanised cities such as Hong Kong, while adding vitality to social experience in achieving deeper understanding and support of heritage conservation and sustainable development.

Key Notes

1. Essential role of rural placemaking and cultural landscapes.
2. Heritage conservation as primarily placekeeping.
3. Leading role of NGOs to preserve and restore historic villages.

References

Centre for Civil Society and Governance. n.d. 'Sustainable Lai Chi Wo: Living Water & Community Revitalization: An Agricultural-led Action, Engagement and Incubation Programme at Lai Chi Wo (2013–2017).' Policy for Sustainability Lab. Accessed 20 March 2025. https://ccsg.hku.hk/ruralsd/en/pages/sustainable-lai-chi-wo-programme-2013-2017/.

5

Transformation of the New Territories and Development of the Nine New Towns

Introduction

In 1972, the Hong Kong government's highest decision-making body, the Governor-in-Council, approved the adoption of a 'Ten-Year Housing Target Programme' that was aimed at providing adequate housing for another 1.8 million people by the mid-1980s (Hong Kong Government 1973, 4). At that time Hong Kong's population was around 4 million, of which only 17% lived in the New Territories, which then was still mainly occupied by farming rural communities consisting mainly of market towns interspersed with original traditional villages.

The objectives for the ten-year public housing programme were set out as follows:

1. To eliminate all squatter and licenced areas;
2. To allow for the redevelopment of cottage areas;
3. To provide self-contained dwellings for all those households presently sharing accommodation in private tenements;
4. To relieve overcrowding in existing government housing, including redevelopment and renovation of the estates where some form of renewal is essential; and
5. To provide housing to those people who have to be rehoused in consequence of other government schemes and policies.

Access to the urban area was difficult. The former Kowloon-Canton Railway only had eighteen services a day (nine in each direction) on a single line track that had many level crossings; the journey from Lo Wu to Kowloon took seventy minutes. The double tracking, electrification, and station modernization you see today was not completed until July 1983.

Similarly for vehicular traffic, there was only an ordinary two-way road system around the New Territories that took all day to navigate.

Now the new 70-kilometre motorway, known as Route 9, circumnavigates the New Territories and was completed in phases from 1985 through to 2007.

The Development Programme

The nine new towns that have been built can be divided into three generations. The first towns, comprising Tsuen Wan, Sha Tin, and Tuen Mun, were started in the early 1970s to help meet the initial housing target which was, broadly speaking achieved, as between 1973 and 1982 they were able to deliver 220,000 flats to house over one million people. These are the three biggest new towns that together now cover some 10,000 hectares of land and house around 2m people.

In the late 1970s the second generation of new towns comprising Tai Po, Fan Ling and Sheung Shui, and Yuen Long were started. These were, in effect, an expansion of three existing traditional market towns which combined now cover over 4,000 hectares of land and house around 750,000 people.

1973 New Town Development Programme

- The first generation of three were Tsuen Wan, Sha Tin and Tuen Mun and were immediately started aiming to provide housing for 1.8 million people.

- These were followed in the late 1970's by the second generation to be built at Tai Po, Fanling/Sheung Shui and Yuen Long.

- The third generation were built at Tseung Kwan O, Tin Shui Wai and Tung Chung in the 1980's and 1990's.

These 9 New Towns now house around 3.4 million people and should rise to 3.5 million by 2018.

Figure 5.1: Nine New Towns – Development Programme – 1973. Photograph courtesy of the New Territories Development Department, PWD (NTDD).

The census figures for 1986 gave Hong Kong's population as 5.5 million, of which 35% were now residing in the New Territories. The third generation comprises Tseung Kwan O, Tin Shui Wai, and Tung Chung and were built in the 1980 and 90s. Tseung Kwan O and Tin Shui Wai are more-or-less completed, occupying slightly over 2,000 hectares and housing some 700,000 people. Tung Chung was one of the previous Airport Core Programme projects built to support the new international airport. Its current population is around 98,000, but there are now plans under way to expand the town both eastwards and westwards with an additional 245 hectares of new land that will be sufficient to provide housing for another 184,000 people.

Between 1976 and 1996, it has been estimated that some 4,000 hectares of this new land was created by reclamations, with the remainder being the subject of land resumptions. As an indication of how government development programs have slowed down, only 1,000 hectares of further reclamation land had been delivered by 2016.

In summary, out of Hong Kong's 2022 total population of 7.5 million, about 3.5 million – or 46.7% – live in the new towns. If you then add back the populations of the established villages and other rural communities from the 2021 Population Census (Census and Statistics Department 2021), 53.7% of the population now live in the New Territories, which – together with all new transport and other infrastructure provisions that have now been put in place – has resulted in this amazing transformation (Civil Engineering and Development Department 2021)! This was placemaking on a grand scale; it is a shame that it effectively came to a standstill after the handover.

The bigger picture impact that all this development activity has had on Hong Kong as a whole can be seen from the 2022 statistics (Census and Statistics Department 2023) on the provision of permanent living quarters by type. Out of a total of 3 million permanent quarters existing in the territory, 858,000 of them (28.6%) are public rental housing units (PRH); 444,000 (14.8%) are subsidized sale flats, and 1.7 million (56.8%) are privately owned. These figures mean that an impressive 43.4% of the total housing stock has, over the years, been provided by the government. However, as discussed later on, there is now an urgent need for more PRH to deal with the unacceptably long waiting list which means that government needs to continue its work.

The Chief Executive Policy Addresses of 2021 and 2022 have announced a return of vigorous government action to help tackle this problem with their visionary plans for the development of the Northern Metropolis (Lam 2021; Lee 2022). These plans are considered in detail in Chapter 6.

Implementation: How Was This Achieved?

At the policy level, the New Territories Development Department (NTDD) was formally set up in 1973 within the former Public Works Department to be responsible for the planning, coordination, and implementation of the development programs of the first generation of new towns.

At the working level, each of the new towns had a Project Manager (PM) in place who was appointed by NTDD. This was invariably a very senior engineer who worked hand in hand with the local District Officer and District Land Officer to plan and implement the new town plan in a timely fashion. These two offices also worked in close conjunction with the Housing Department so that land acquisition and clearance were implemented in the sequence required for the engineering and building programmes. The PM also needed to coordinate the work of the utility companies to ensure the timely provision of their services to the new land being created.

In view of the vast and wide-ranging amount of engineering work that needed to be carried out efficiently, the PMs employed private consultant engineers to assist them in this work.

Concurrently, the Planning Branch was upgraded to a full-fledged office within the Lands, Survey, and Town Planning Department operating under the umbrella of the Public Works Department. In its first year, it completed the statutory Outline Zoning Plans (OZPs) for Tsuen Wan/Kwai Chung and Sha Tin.

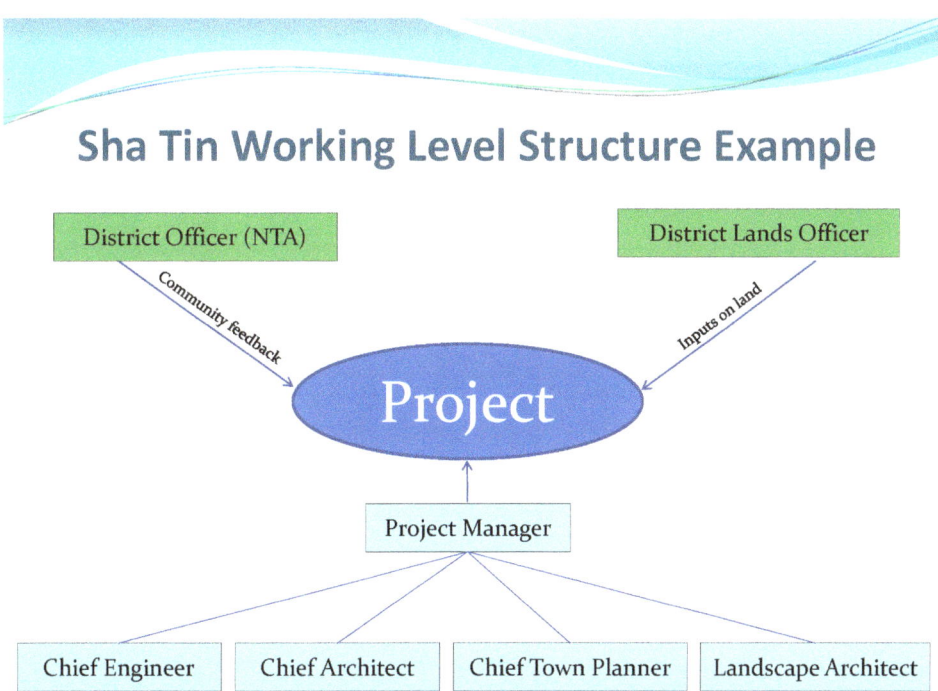

Figure 5.2: Working Level Structure example. Photograph courtesy of the New Territories Development Department, PWD (NTDD).

This was followed in subsequent years by a further seven OZPs for the majority of the remaining new towns. The preparation of these OZPs was a vital part of the implementation process – it enabled the District Officers to carry out their important consultation work with the local community in order to gain their support for the new plan, as well as allowed the District Land Officers to proceed with the required land resumption and clearance of any private land involved that was needed for the implementation of such OZPs. Under the former Crown Land Resumption Ordinance, such land resumptions could only proceed with the authority of the Governor-in-Council who needed to be satisfied that such resumptions were for a 'public purpose'. In these cases, the provision of public housing as part of the implementation of the OZP and the Ten-Year Housing Target Programme were clearly a public purpose; nevertheless, the process still needed to be respected and followed. The then governor, Murray MacLehose, was the driving force behind the initial new town development programme and he made sure that the whole of government was behind him. He was Hong Kong's longest serving governor from 1971–1982. In recognition of the many significant contributions he made to the territory, he was knighted in 1976 and, on retirement, elevated as a life peer to the House of Lords in 1983.

Today, the process and procedure remain the same, although the word 'crown' has, understandably, been removed from the legislative title; the authority for approval now rests with the Chief Executive-in-Council. For the first decade of this work, the government committed enormous sums of money for the physical construction work, but it devised a unique system of compensation for the compulsory acquisition and resumption of the huge tracts of land needed for each New Town, thus avoiding another large outlay of cash that it would have struggled to cope with. This was called the Letter A/B system (Nissim 2022, 123–28) whereby the government issued what was, in effect, a promissory note in respect of a future grant of land. The terms of each Letter A/B conferred upon the holder an entitlement to a grant at an unspecified future date for building land by exchange at a ratio specified in the document.

The vast majority of land resumed was in agricultural status, and the exchange ratio was usually two square feet (0.19 square metres) of building land for every five square feet (0.46 square metres) of agricultural land. For building land, the exchange ratio was one to one. This method of compensation was hugely popular with the New Territories landowners as it created, in effect, a futures market in land, so the villagers were able sell their Letters A/B on the open market to developers and profit that way. At one stage, the government had accumulated an outstanding commitment of 36 million square feet (roughly 3.3 million square metres); as a result, the system had to be stopped in 1983 and was replaced by a generous ex gratia cash compensation package.

Four developers, namely Sun Hung Kai Properties, Henderson Land Development, New World Development, and the Chinachem Group became the principal buyers of large numbers of these Letters A/B, which then enabled them to participate in the government land tenders designed specifically to redeem the outstanding commitment. In order to meet this commitment, 75% of all government land sales in the New Towns each year were designated for this purpose, enabling the four companies to establish a firm foothold in the development of the New Territories. The first three mentioned are all publicly listed companies. The experience and knowledge they gained by engaging in the operation of the Letter A/B system stood them in good stead as they were, after the Letter A/B land sale system ceased in 1996, able to carry all this local activity forward. By gaining detailed knowledge of how land matters in the New Territories operated, working with a network of agents established to assist them in the purchase of the Letters A/B, and mobilizing the contacts they made with the local village representatives and leaders, they were able to assemble significant land banks of primarily agricultural land suitable for their ongoing development programmes, which cemented their position as the leading property developers in the both the New Territories and Hong Kong as a whole. By way of example, Sun Hung Kai were able to execute a major land exchange in 2017 at Shap Sze Heung comprising about 62 hectares, or 6.67 million square feet, for residential development and other facilities, paying a premium of close to HK$16 billion.

'The Best Laid Plans!'

The full quotation comes from a Robert Burns poem, which translated from Scots reads: 'The best laid plans of mice and men often go awry.' This certainly applies to the planning of the first two generations of new towns, which were envisaged to be self-contained communities that provided a full range of affordable rental and home ownership housing, shopping and commercial space, schools, hospitals, recreational facilities, as well as factory space in order for there to be sufficient local employment opportunities for the adult population.

In their defence, the planners could not possibly have anticipated the huge impact Deng Xiaoping's 'Open Door Policy' would have once it was launched in 1979. This ground-breaking initiative resulted in the establishment of the Pearl River Delta Economic Zone, which was to encourage export-oriented production by foreign-invested entities based in Shenzhen, Dongguan, and Guangzhou. Hong Kong manufacturers were quick to seize the opportunity to access cheap land, cheap labour, and preferential tax policies and relocate their clock and watch, toy, made-up garment, plastic, and textile operations across the border, thereby contributing to the establishment and growth of the Pearl River Delta Economic Zone.

These manufacturers had the benefit of being able to continue living in Hong Kong and commute across the border to their factories as necessary, while usually retaining their headquarters function in Hong Kong to handle the import/export matters, design, finance, and insurance as well as quality control. The result was that very quickly, Hong Kong transitioned from a manufacturing-based economy to a service-based economy. This led to a rapid decline in demand for factory space and a surging demand for high quality office space from

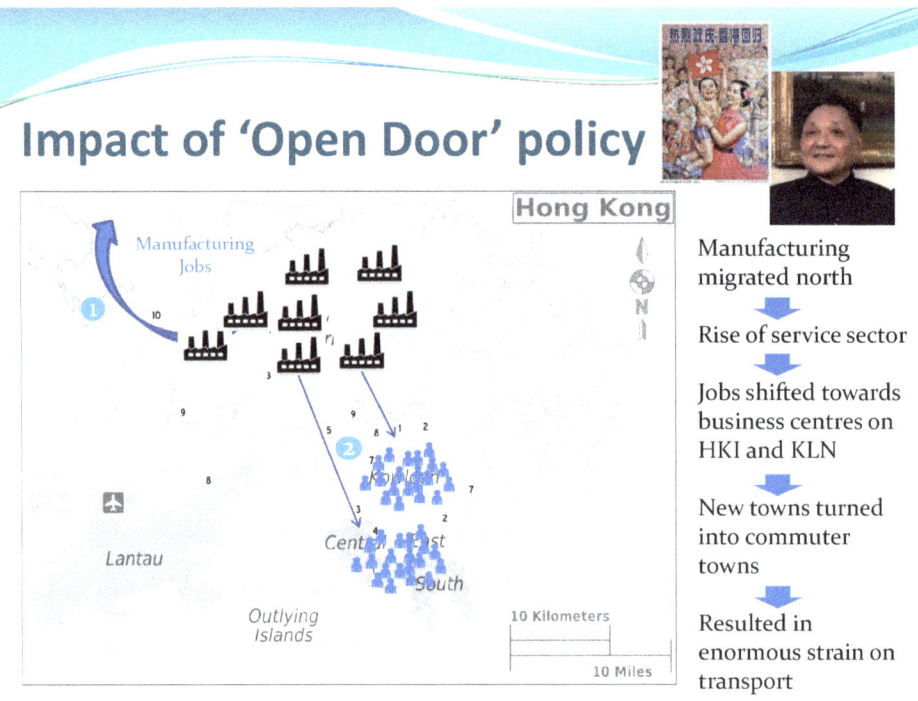

Figure 5.3: Impact of the 'Open Door' Policy. Photograph courtesy of the New Territories Development Department, PWD (NTDD).

the boom in new service industries. Over the past five years, these services have consistently contributed 92–93% to our GDP with activities such as import and export, wholesale, and retail trades, with finance and insurance being the highest contributors.

Prior to the establishment of the Pearl River Delta Economic Zone, it was estimated that there were about 800,000 people working in Hong Kong-based factories, but once they moved and expanded their operations into the Economic Zone, it was estimated that this figure grew to 10 to 12 million people employed in Hong Kong owned factories. This gives a measure of the expansion of business that then needed to be serviced.

Because of this change in economic drivers, the new towns rapidly became more like dormitory towns, as most of the employment opportunities were found in the business districts on Hong Kong Island and in Kowloon. This unplanned-for event resulted in a huge burden on the public transport system, which the government has spent the last two decades trying to accommodate and remedy.

It is only Tung Chung, which was built as one of the Airport Core Projects in the 1990s, that enjoyed the benefit of proper road and rail access right from the start. All the other new towns have needed retrofitting of either (or both) road or rail connections to meet all the changes in travel demand. This work is still ongoing and the eastern side of the New Territories could only be considered complete when the MTR's Sha Tin to Central Link, after much delay, was finally opened in the summer of 2022.

What Comes Next? The New Development Areas

Even though previous planning and development studies dating back to the 1990s had established the feasibility of developing New Development Areas (NDA's) in the New Territories, it wasn't until the Hong Kong 2030 Planning and Vision Strategy (Planning Department 2016) was promulgated in 2007 that a decision was made to proceed with these NDAs at Kwu Tung North, Fan Ling North, Hung Shui Kiu and Ha Tsuen, and Kam Tin South, together with the expansion of Tung Chung West already mentioned. This was followed in 2008 by a lengthy public engagement exercise that was not completed until 2013, which then enabled the statutory planning process and detailed design to be done. Land resumption has been slow to follow. Only in the Chief Executive's 2019 policy address was there any sense of urgency injected into the process when it was announced that 700 hectares of private land would be resumed, of which 400 hectares is expected to be resumed in the next five years for the implementation of these NDAs. It should be noted that in the five years prior to this announcement, a mere 20 hectares had been resumed. In addition, there are an estimated 450 hectares of brownfield sites that have not been included in the NDAs; the Planning Department was charged with an urgent review of these sites to assess their suitability for public housing development by inclusion into adjacent NDAs.

On 24 March 2021 the Secretary for Development, Michael Wong, reported in a written reply to the Legislative Council that government had followed through on its commitment to expedite these projects having, in the previous two years, resumed some 90 hectares of land out of which 80 hectares were for the NDAs and intended for PRH. Looking ahead, he said about 700 hectares of land, including 600 hectares for the NDAs, will be resumed from 2021 to 2022; of this, around 500 hectares will be resumed in the coming five years with 400 hectares for PRH. He also reported that the Planning Department's review of brownfield sites had, as at the end of 2020, identified 160 hectares of such land as having high development potential and a further 290 hectares having medium potential. As these sites are situated mainly on private land, they will require resumption once the planning and engineering procedures have been completed.

As a result of all these activities, the 2020 Policy Address was able to lay out an ambitious plan that demonstrated a clear pivot towards the production of PRH in the coming ten years with a seventy-to-thirty split between public and private housing production. Previously, the target split had been sixty-to-forty for the planning of new towns. This change was necessary since the average waiting time for the 150,000 general applications for PRH has increased from 4.6 years in 2017 to 5.8 years in 2021 – far above the accepted norm of 3 years.

The Long-Term Housing Strategy, which was first promulgated in 2014, has since been subject to updated annual progress reports. The latest report in 2022 reconfirmed the seventy-to-thirty split between public and private housing for the ten-year period 2023–2024 to 2032–2033 with a total supply target of 430,000 units; 301,000 for public housing and 129,000 for private housing (Housing Bureau 2022).

Quite a number of developers have their own land banks which they could draw from should they feel the supply from the government is insufficient.

These NDAs have the potential to deliver at least 180,000 new flats whose numbers, both for land supply and flat production, are significantly smaller than those for the existing new towns.

The proposed plot ratios for the NDAs are generally less than five in comparison to the new towns, which had a five to eight plot ratio. Given the amount of time spent in getting to the land resumption stage, there is a very good case for these plot ratios to be reviewed and raised so that the government and the public can get the best value out of the new land. The land resumption and clearance costs are the same whether the land acquired is built to three, five, or seven plot ratio; given the flat supply shortage, surely the government has a duty and responsibility to maximize the use of this land as far as possible.

Apart from Tung Chung, all the other NDAs mentioned above will be subsumed into and form an important part of the ambitious plans for the Northern Metropolis considered in Chapter 6.

Sha Tin New Town

In 1977, Sha Tin's Outline Development Plan set out the following aspirational objectives with the target of achieving self-containment:

(1) to create a balanced and vigorous self-contained community to meet the basic needs of all the residents;
(2) to provide new opportunities and freedom of choice for residents in location, type, standard of housing, education, and employment;
(3) to create a meaningful community to which people can relate healthily with a strong sense of place and where people can develop socially, and;
(4) to provide ease, safety, and convenience of movement for residents to and from their place of work, learning, shopping, and recreation; to use available resources efficiently, wisely, and imaginatively; and to create an attractive and convenient city appropriate to the district.

With the exception of 'to provide ease and convenience of movement for residents to and from their place of work', which has been discussed in previous paragraphs, the above objectives have, by and large, been met. The 2021 census showed that only 12.35% of the

Sha Tin: Then & Now

1978

2012

Figure 5.4: Shatin: Then (1978) and now (2012). Photograph reproduced by permission from Hong Kong Map Service 2.0, Lands Department.

Sha Tin: Then & Now

1986

2013

Figure 5.5: Shatin: Then (1986) and now (2013). Photograph reproduced by permission from Hong Kong Map Service 2.0, Lands Department.

Sha Tin working population's place of work was in the same district. The total population for Sha Tin and Ma On Shan combined at the time of the 2021 census was given as 692,806 (Census and Statistics Department 2021); before all the new town development started, the population was around 30,000.

Looking at the census figures for Sha Tin and Ma On Shan as a whole, PRH provides 32.4% of the housing units, subsidized sale flats 25.17%, and private housing 42.43%. Interestingly, when Ma On Shan, which was built later in the 1980s and 90s as an extension to Sha Tin, the emphasis had changed to encourage more home ownership; this is reflected in their figures showing an unusually low 15% of PRH, a huge 43% of subsidized sale flats, and 42% private housing.

Figure 5.6: Typical public housing – Shek Mun, Shatin. Photograph courtesy of Steven847 on Wikipedia.

Examples of Private Housing

City One Shatin (High Rise)

Kau To Shan (Low Rise)

Figure 5.7: Examples of private housing. Photograph courtesy of Steven847 on Wikipedia.

Similar to the other first- and second-generation new towns, Sha Tin was planned on the basis of a maximum residential plot ratio of five, whereas the third-generation new towns, including Ma On Shan, were allowed to go up to a maximum plot ratio of eight.

In the 2021 census, the median monthly domestic household income of economically active households in Sha Tin was HK$36,170 compared with the territory wide median average of HK$28,300; the proportion of domestic households owning their own quarters was 54.8% compared with the territory wide average of 48.6%. These snapshots of data give an indication of the nature, balance, and quality of the community that has evolved here.

One key feature in the planning of Sha Tin was the design and development of the town centre, based on Yuncken Freeman's 1982 detailed site design that they completed as consultant architects to the Project Manager Sha Tin, which provided for a large single-use retail centre and transport-oriented circulation hub for the new town centre.

The design was translated into a set of detailed control drawings that formed part of the tender conditions when the site now known as New Town Plaza – a shopping and office complex of around one million square feet (roughly 92,900 square metres) gross floor area – was tendered for sale by the government in 1983 through the Letter A/B system referred to above and acquired by Sun Hung Kai. The control drawings stipulated development

New Town Plaza -1982 Design Model

Figure 5.8: New Town Plaza Design Model – 1982. Photograph courtesy of Yuncken Freeman.

Figure 5.9: New Town Plaza Today. Photograph courtesy of Sun Hung Kai Properties.

parameters such as construction and linking of the shopping podiums with pre-determined levels and boundaries that ensured the permeability and accessibility of the space for the public within the shopping centre. The relatively low-rise character of the building was planned to smooth pedestrian movement from the train station to adjacent estates, cultural amenities, and open spaces. The site sits above a major public transport interchange and immediately adjacent to Sha Tin MTR station and has now become the recognized regional shopping centre for this part of the New Territories. There are six adjoining developments – four with shopping and commercial podiums with residential towers above, one with an office tower, and one hotel. All of these developments had lease requirements to provide covered, elevated, public pedestrian passages that would interlink with each other through to New Town Plaza. Similarly, the nearby public buildings such as Sha Tin Town Hall, Shatin Law Courts Building, and Sha Tin Public Library are also linked to this elevated pedestrian network so that the town centre has become an interconnected whole. This integration of both public and private sector developments has resulted in the creation of a genuine 'Civic Heart' for Sha Tin as referenced in Figures 5.10 and 5.11 below (Tan and Xue 2016).

The basic lesson had been well learned from the elevated pedestrian network in Central, but with the enormous benefit of having a 'clean slate' of new land, all the sites that make up the town centre were sold with lease requirements to ensure they provided dedicated, interconnected, pedestrian-friendly gallerias, skywalks, and podium terraces that would offer a visual and physical human scale environment for the benefit of the public. In effect, this arrangement initiated the privatization of Hong Kong's public space in the commercial districts, which was then followed in the later developments of Hong Kong and Kowloon Station sites for the Airport Railway. The big benefit of privatizing the management of such public open spaces is that the private sector is much better equipped and has more flexibility to deal with all the ongoing placekeeping aspects that these areas require in a timely manner, such as the regular management, upkeep, and improvements that over time will inevitably be needed, given that they are not hide bound by bureaucratic rules, regulations, and financing procedures by which public sector managers would be constrained.

Sha Tin is fortunate to have within its boundaries the Chinese University of Hong Kong (CUHK) and the associated medical teaching Prince of Wales Hospital. It also has three international hotels, including one at CUHK, the Hyatt Regency Teaching Hotel, with 567 rooms designed for acquiring hands-on experience by the students of the Hotel Management Programme run jointly with Cornell University, New York. Having this wide range of facilities within its boundaries all helps to give Sha Tin that important balance to the make-up of its community. Although technically falling within Tai Po district, the Hong Kong Science and Technology Park is located immediately adjacent to CUHK and is far better connected to Sha Tin than Tai Po, which adds more value all round to Sha Tin.

Sha Tin was not an easy place to plan; being surrounded on three sides by hills with the Shing Mun River going down the middle, it was unavoidably linear in design. Quite a few

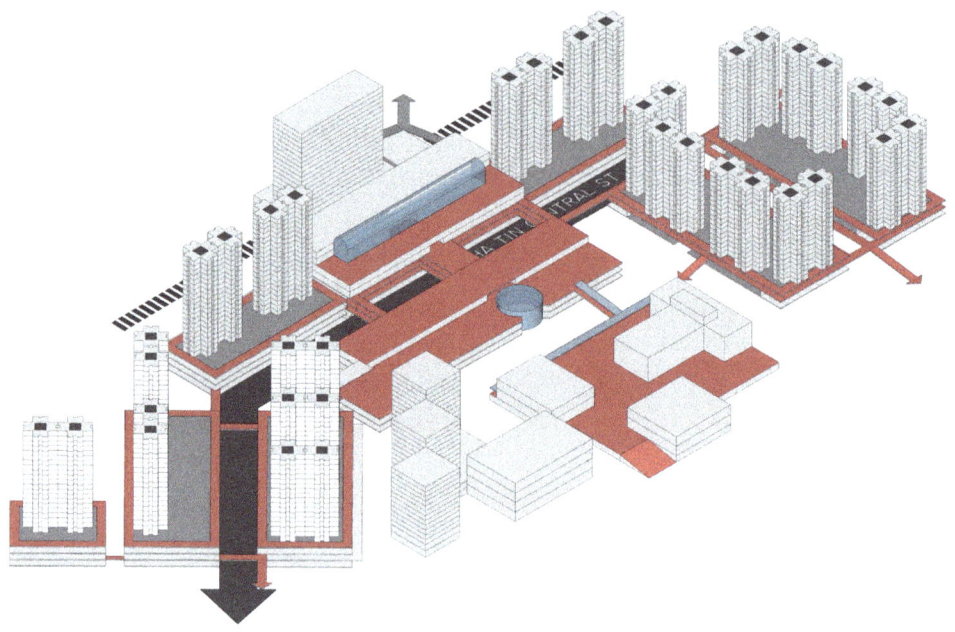

Figure 5.10: Pedestrian Connectivity Plan. Illustration courtesy of Yuncken Freeman.

Figure 5.11: Pedestrian connectivity as built. Photographs courtesy of Yuncken Freeman.

Figure 5.12: Tin Sum Village – Tai Wai, with Lung Hang Estate in the foreground and Festival City in the background. Photograph courtesy of WiNG 1990hk on Wikimedia Commons.

Figure 5.13: Tsang Tai Uk. Photograph courtesy of CPJoseph on Wikimedia Commons.

of the original traditional villages such as Tin Sam and the walled village of Tsang Tai Uk, shown above, were retained within the new town layout, giving some welcome low-rise, low-density relief and contrast to the new, predominantly high-rise urban landscape.

The surrounding hills are part of local country parks, which means the residents have convenient and easy access to good quality countryside for both walking and hiking. The reconfigured Shing Mun River has a 3,000-metre stretch of water that is now home to the Sha Tin Rowing Centre; it is highly suitable for international rowing events that local rowers participate in and train for, such as the Olympic Games and Asian Games. On either side of the river, there are shaded pedestrian and cycle tracks several kilometres long for local recreation. In fact, you can now walk, jog, or cycle all the way from Tai Wai to Ma On Shan on a very pleasant dedicated waterfront trail past the Hong Kong Heritage Museum, Sha Tin Park, and the Hong Kong Sports Institute. The Sha Tin Racecourse enables the locals to enjoy the popular pastime of horse racing in a most convenient way. All these are in addition to the many public parks and open spaces that have been provided such that the overall density of population, which for Sha Tin in 2021 stood at 9,994 persons per square kilometre – well below that of the urban areas of Hong Kong Island (averaging 14,960) and Kowloon (averaging 47,560). This all helps add to the quality of life that goes a long way to achieving the 1977 planning objectives.

References

Census and Statistics Department, Hong Kong SAR Government. 2021. '2021 Census'. https://www.censtatd.gov.hk/en/scode600.html.

Census and Statistics Department, Hong Kong SAR Government. 2023. 'Hong Kong in Figures 2023'. https://www.censtatd.gov.hk/en/EIndexbySubject.html?scode=460&pcode=B1010006.

Civil Engineering and Development Department. 2021. *Hong Kong: The Facts – New Development Areas and Urban Developments*. https://www.gov.hk/en/about/abouthk/factsheets/docs/towns_urban_developments.pdf.

Housing Bureau. 2022. *Long Term Housing Strategy: Annual Progress Report 2022 (for the 10-Year Period from 2023–24 to 2032–33)*. https://www.hb.gov.hk/eng/policy/housing/policy/lths/LTHS_Annual_Progress_Report_2022.pdf.

Information Services Department. 1973. *Hong Kong 1973, Report for the Year 1972*. Hong Kong Government Press.

Lam, Carrie. 2019. 'The Chief Executive's 2019 Policy Address.' Policy Address. https://www.policyaddress.gov.hk/2019/eng/policy.html.

Lam, Carrie. 2020. 'The Chief Executive's 2020 Policy Address.' Policy Address. https://www.policyaddress.gov.hk/2020/eng/policy.html.

Lam, Carrie. 2021. 'The Chief Executive's 2021 Policy Address.' Policy Address. https://www.policyaddress.gov.hk/2021/eng/policy.html.

Lee, John. 2022. 'The Chief Executive's 2022 Policy Address.' Policy Address. https://www.policyaddress.gov.hk/2022/en/policy.html.

Nissim, Roger. 2022. *Land Administration and Practice in Hong Kong*. Fifth edition. Hong Kong University Press.

Planning Department, Hong Kong SAR Government. 2016. *Hong Kong 2030+: Towards a Planning and Vision and Strategy Transcending 2030*. Archived 19 February, 2023 at https://web.archive.org/web/20230219111620/https://www.pland.gov.hk/pland_en/p_study/comp_s/hk2030plus/document/2030+Booklet_Eng.pdf.

Secretary for Development, Hong Kong SAR Government. 2021. 'LCQ15: Private land suitable for public housing development'. Press Releases. https://www.devb.gov.hk/en/publications_and_press_releases/press/index_id_10902.html.

Tan, Zheng, and Charlie Q. L. Xue. 2016. 'The Evolution of an Urban Vision: The Multilevel Pedestrian Networks in Hong Kong, 1965–1997.' *Journal of Urban History* 42 (4): 688–708.

Acknowledgements

The two b/w aerial photos no. 21052, 1978 and A04916, 1986 shown on the plate 'Sha Tin Then & Now' on page 71, are provided by the CSDI portal and the intellectual property rights are owned by the Government of the HKSAR. The two coloured aerial photos, dated 2012 and 2013 shown on the same plate, page 71, are reproduced with permission of the Director of Lands, © The Government of the Hong Kong SAR. Licence No. 32/2023.

The Government Information Services Department has given permission to use the other aerial photographs.

New Towns in the New Territories: Commentary (NC)

In *The City of To-morrow and Its Planning* (1929), the legendary architect Le Corbusier boldly proposed an unprecedented vision for modern cities, highlighted by the iconic perspective drawing of high-rise cruciform towers surrounded by landscaped parks and his prototypical Plan Voisin for Paris. His urban strategy was to build densely in the urban centres and preserve open land for recreation. The post-World War II urban development of Hong Kong is arguably the most faithful realisation of this vision. A side-by-side comparison of the Plan Voisin and Mei Foo Sun Chuen in Kowloon (1968–1978) resembles before-and-after images of building model and built reality.

In the modern urban development of Hong Kong, the built-over land is only 24% (Civil Engineering and Development Department, HKSAR 2019). Country Parks account for about 40% of total land area even after the extensive planning and development of NDAs in the New Territories. These new towns have realized placemaking at the mega-scale of urban and regional planning. But why has the premise of Le Corbusier been largely successful in Hong Kong and not in other nations? Pruit-Igoe in St Louis and Cabrini-Green in Chicago

Figure 5.14: Le Corbusier: Plan Voisin in Paris. Photograph courtesy of Amber Case.

Figure 5.15: Mei Foo Sun Chuen. Photograph courtesy of Wong Tung & Partners.

The Transformation of the New Territories 81

Figure 5.16: Aerial view of Sha Tin. Photograph by Panther Media, Alamy.

are just two infamous examples of high-rise public housing projects in the US among countless others that declined into poverty-stricken slums and ultimately were demolished respectively in the mid-1970s and mid-2000s.

In contrast, the exemplary example of urban planning and design of new town developments in Hong Kong have been the subject of academic research overseas (Paint Square 2013; Zacharias 2005). The difference for Hong Kong, according to the late Tunney Lee, professor and founding chair of the CUHK School of Architecture, was higher density – not lower density – as well as placemaking. In the American examples, so-called public housing 'projects' were isolated from their cities; residents needed to leave their projects to reach shops, clinics, and other amenities. No one from outside the projects entered except for its own residents.

In Hong Kong, however, living densities are sufficiently high for public housing estates to be augmented and integrated with convenience shopping and community centres, as well as open space for leisure and recreation. Other city residents will also access these estates for amenities not found in their own estates.

At the next urban scale, the housing estates in NDAs are in close vicinity to major town facilities including schools, hospitals, civic facilities and recreational parks. Thus, they are not simply residential blocks but also community-scaled places within the larger urban network of Hong Kong.

Key Notes

1. Vision of *The City of To-morrow and Its Planning* is more fully realised in Hong Kong than elsewhere.
2. Higher density, not lower density, enables housing estates to be communities.
3. Placemaking at the scale of housing estates and town centres.

References

Civil Engineering and Development Department. 2019. 'Information Sheet 2: Land Usage Distribution in Hong Kong.' Archived 9 November, 2019 at https://web.archive.org/web/20191109104932/https://www.cedd.gov.hk/filemanager/eng/content_954/Info_Sheet2.pdf.

Paint Square. 2013. 'Rice University to Study China's New Towns.' https://www.paintsquare.com/news/view/?10441/.

Zacharias, John. 2005. 'Generating Urban Lifestyle: The Case of Hong Kong New Town Design and Local Travel Behaviour.' *Journal of Urban Design* 10 (3): 371–86. https://doi.org/10.1080/13574800500297843.

6

The Future: Northern Metropolis Development Strategy

Background

The Northern Metropolis Development Strategy (NMDS) was first introduced in the Chief Executive Carrie Lam's policy address of October 2021 and represents the most meaningful, ambitious, and positive evolution of territorial land use planning this millennium. If fully realized, it will become a genuine example of future 'placemaking'. To give a sense of the scale of this plan – it will impact some 30,000 hectares of land across the Yuen Long and North Districts of the New Territories.

Following the implementation of economic reforms and the opening-up policy of mainland China in 1978, and the subsequent establishment of the Shenzhen Special Economic Zone and the Pearl River Delta Open Economic Zone, Hong Kong forged very close economic ties with mainland China, particularly in the Pearl River Delta region.

During the same period of time, Hong Kong's key industries also underwent transformation from light industries to financial and service industries as the basis. Prior to the outbreak of COVID-19, Hong Kong had leveraged national policies to become the springboard for international capital and enterprises to enter mainland China and for mainland enterprises to gain access to international markets. As such, Hong Kong was able to develop into an international financial centre performing these unique functions. Hopefully, as the hiatus of the past three years starts to fade, Hong Kong will be able to re-establish this pivotal role.

The NMDS fully recognizes the significance of these changes such that, for the first time, the plan not only builds on the Planning Department's 'Hong Kong 2030+: Towards a Planning Vision and Strategy Transcending 2030' (2016) but also makes reference to China's plan for Hong Kong to become an International Innovation and Technical hub (outlined in

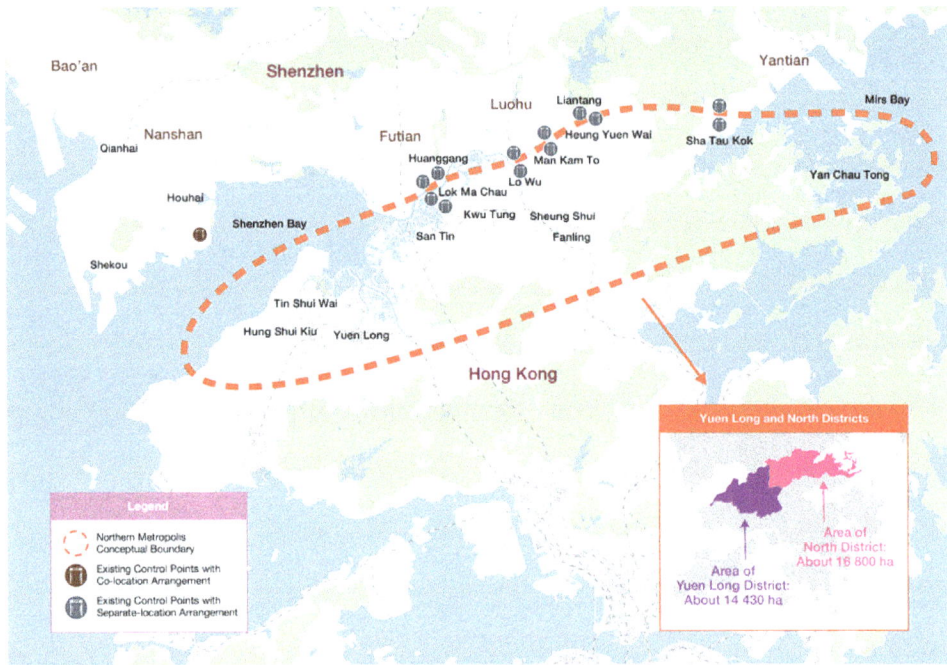

Figure 6.1: Northern Metropolis Development Strategy Area. Reproduced by permission from the Development Bureau. ©2022 Development Bureau, Government of the Hong Kong Special Administrative Region of the People's Republic of China.

the National 14th Five-Year Plan), as well as the Outline Development Plan for the Greater Bay Area comprising Guangdong Province, Hong Kong, and Macau.

In October 2022, the incoming Chief Executive John Lee's first policy address reaffirmed the government's commitment to the NMDS. Under the heading 'Fully and faithfully implement "One Country, Two Systems"' is the statement to 'Integrate into national development by pressing ahead with strategic projects, including the Northern Metropolis' (Lee 2022). To help achieve this, the Chief Executive himself will adopt a top-down, hands-on approach creating and leading a new Steering Committee that will provide high-level policy supervision. The development of the Northern Metropolis is seen as the primary engine for growth for Hong Kong. All the above guiding principles were reiterated in Lee's October 2023 policy address and we now await the details of the implementation of the new 'industry-driven and infrastructure led' approach (Lee 2023) which, hopefully, will give due regard to the six planning principles set out below.

In the past 40 years or so, a wide-spread agglomeration of cities has emerged along the east and west banks of the Pearl River. Hong Kong has continuously intensified its interaction with this region, and particularly with Shenzhen. For Hong Kong, Shenzhen is the gateway to the hinterland of the Greater Bay Area by land and rail transport. The number of Hong Kong and Shenzhen residents commuting between the two cities every day for leisure, visiting relatives, business, work, and school has ever been increasing. For example, according to the Immigration Department's figures Lo Wu Control Point was the busiest control point before the outbreak of COVID-19 with daily average passenger count of 260,000. An integrated development pattern characterized by the close intertwining of Hong Kong and Shenzhen has been formed and the NMDS aims to build and improve upon this. This represents a welcome 'paradigm shift in respect of mode of thinking for Hong Kong-Shenzhen co-operation, spatial concept, policy formulation, and institutional establishment' underlying the proposed action items; the action items include creating more environmental capacity, cross-boundary ecological corridors, resumption of land necessary for conservation, and the effective realization and efficient execution of this bold strategy. The vision is for innovation and technology industries (I&T) to become the economic engine for this area. Closer liaison with Shenzhen will help Hong Kong develop as they have already demonstrated, with their opening up, high capability in self-reliant innovation which, hopefully, we can harness and supplement. The establishment of the Office for Attracting Strategic Enterprises was proposed in the 2022 policy address with the intention of working and collaborating with the Hongkong-Shenzhen Innovation and Technology Park as well as attracting high-quality enterprises and talents to Hong Kong and would primarily focus on industries such as life and health technology, artificial intelligence, and data science.

Shenzhen's economy surpassed Hong Kong's for the first time in 2018 with 5.46% of its GDP being devoted to research and development compared with Hong Kong's 2020 equivalent figure of 1%. Clearly, Hong Kong has some catching up to do in this regard.

Hong Kong has a number of advantages such as top-notch universities and science institutions in areas such as artificial intelligence and biotechnology with, for example, vaccine development and drug discovery. In addition, the city gives important financial support to the industry as a financial hub, raising capital and legal services to companies seeking to be listed on the local stock exchange. The investor base here, rule of law, and access to international markets will all help the city enhance both its and Shenzhen's I&T industries.

To help underline the importance of Hong Kong's contribution to this vision, data and infrastructure company Refinitiv reports that ever since Hong Kong Exchanges and Clearing introduced listing reforms in 2018, the city has become the favourite fundraising hub for technology-related companies, with 93 biotechnology firms collecting HK$258.5 billion in fresh capital. They further reported that 98% of fundraising via IPOs in Hong Kong in 2021 came from mainland Chinese companies.

NMDS Planning Principles

There are six planning principles which should be studied carefully, as they clearly show the new thinking and direction behind this strategy:

(1) Urban-rural integration: The Northern Metropolis will be created with a unique metropolitan landscape featuring 'Urban-Rural Integration and Co-existence of Development and Conservation'.
(2) Proactive conservation: Proactive conservation measures should be adopted to expand environmental capacity, preserve the integrity of strategic ecological corridors, guard against damage to the ecosystem by unauthorized developments, and reasonably compensate for the environmental impact of development activities.
(3) High-quality outdoor eco-recreation/tourism outlets: In anticipation of a considerable growth of the residential and working population in the Northern Metropolis, quality outdoor eco-recreation and tourism outlets of high landscape value should be created in a timely manner.
(4) Optimized spatial planning for economic land: Planning and design for economic land should be optimized. Proactive measures should be taken to attract I&T enterprises in the industrial chain to establish businesses in the Northern Metropolis in order to provide local employment opportunities, thus improving the home-job spatial distribution.
(5) Expansion of development capacity: More land that is suitable for development should be identified. The development nodes and corridors connecting various border crossing points should be expanded to tackle the problem of shortage in land and housing supply.
(6) Enhancing the efficiency, capacity, and comfort level of cross-boundary travel: More cross-boundary transport infrastructure and customs clearance services should be optimized, strengthened, and provided. The Hong Kong-Shenzhen One-hour Cross-boundary Commuting Network should be created to expand the connectivity between Hong Kong and Shenzhen.

The first three planning principles set out above demonstrate the vision to create, for the first time in Hong Kong, a unique metropolitan landscape aiming for the co-existence of development and conservation. We should all welcome and support this exciting and holistic approach to strategic planning which, if properly executed, will deliver a good city for people to live in, work and travel.

From 'Two Bays, One River' to 'Twin Cities, Three Circles'

The NMDS shows us how the existing seven land-based border crossing points and west-to-east transport infrastructure of Hong Kong and Shenzhen have connected the two cities across the Shenzhen River between Shenzhen Bay and Mirs Bay, in effect dissolving the old boundary between the two cities so that they have now created between themselves a special framework of 'Twin Cities, Three Circles'. To identify them and elaborate:

1. Shenzhen Bay Quality Development Circle:

- Upgrading the Hung Shui Kiu/Ha Tsuen New Developments Area (NDA) into the New Territories North central business district, creating more jobs for the new economy.
- Developing a rail link between Hung Shui Kiu and Qianhai and implementing co-location arrangements at Qianhai.
- Conserving and improving wetlands and mangroves inside the circle.

2. Hong Kong-Shenzhen Close Interaction Circle:

- Facilitating development of the San Tin Technopole and establishing a complete I&T industry ecosystem.
- Optimizing, strengthening, and providing more cross-boundary transport infrastructure in the Circle with a view to developing a seamless, convenient, and diversified cross-boundary transport network.
- Creating environmental capacity with enhanced ecological value and developing an ecological habitat network by taking advantage of the extensive stretch of fishponds and wetlands.

3. Mirs Bay/Yan Chau Tong Eco-recreation/Tourism Circle:

- Conserving and enhancing the Circle's overall natural landscape, ecology, and habitat resources.
- Creating opportunities for sustainable eco-recreation and tourism so as to provide a rich array of leisure options for residents of Hong Kong and Shenzhen.

Highlights of Action Items

1) San Tin Technopole

- With an area of 1,100 hectares, it will be planned as an integrated community in order to attract I&T talents to settle there for working and living. Fully developed, it can provide floor space over sixteen times greater than the existing Hong Kong Science and Technology Park.

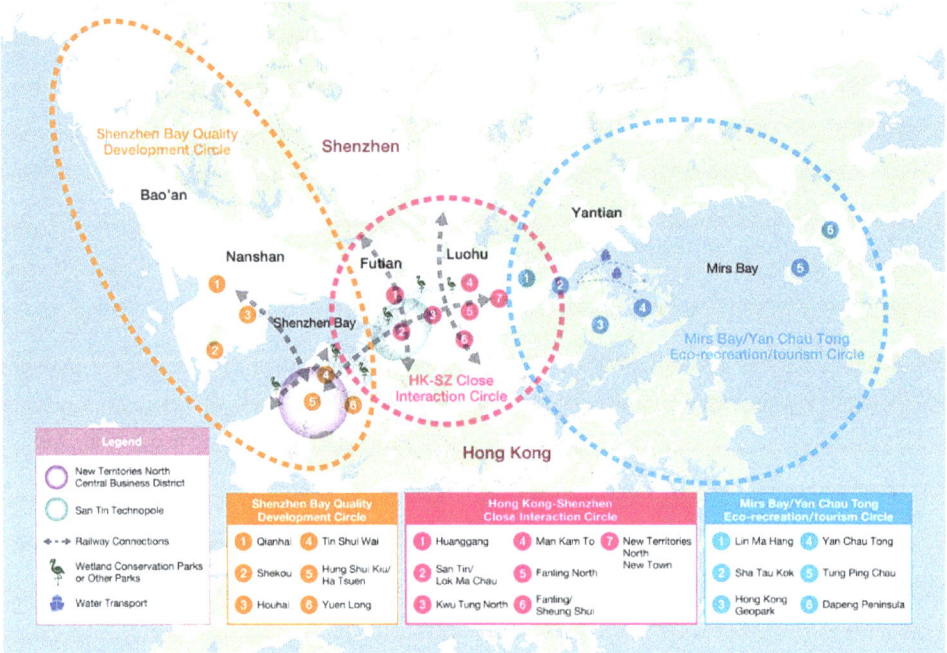

Figure 6.2: Twin Cities, Three Circles. Reproduced by permission from the Development Bureau. ©2022 Development Bureau, Government of the Hong Kong Special Administrative Region of the People's Republic of China.

- In fact, Phase 1 development of the Hong Kong-Shenzhen Innovation and Technology Park is now under construction on the Lok Ma Chau Loop, which will provide in total 87 hectares of land for I&T use, potentially accommodating 50,000 jobs. This development should also be able to accommodate station facilities for the proposed Northern Link (NOL) Spur Line, which will be a cross-boundary railway that will further strengthen direct transport links between the two cities.

2) Outdoor Eco-recreation/Tourism Space Projects

- New Territories North Urban-Rural Greenway that traverses the countryside and penetrates into urban areas.
- Coastal Protection Park and waterfront promenade from Tsim Bei Tsui to Pak Nai.

3) Wetland Conservation Parks

- Nam Sang Wai Wetland Conservation Park (about 400 hectares)
- Sam Po Shue Wetland Conservation Park (about 520 hectares)
- Hoo Hok Wai Wetland Conservation Park (about 300 hectares)

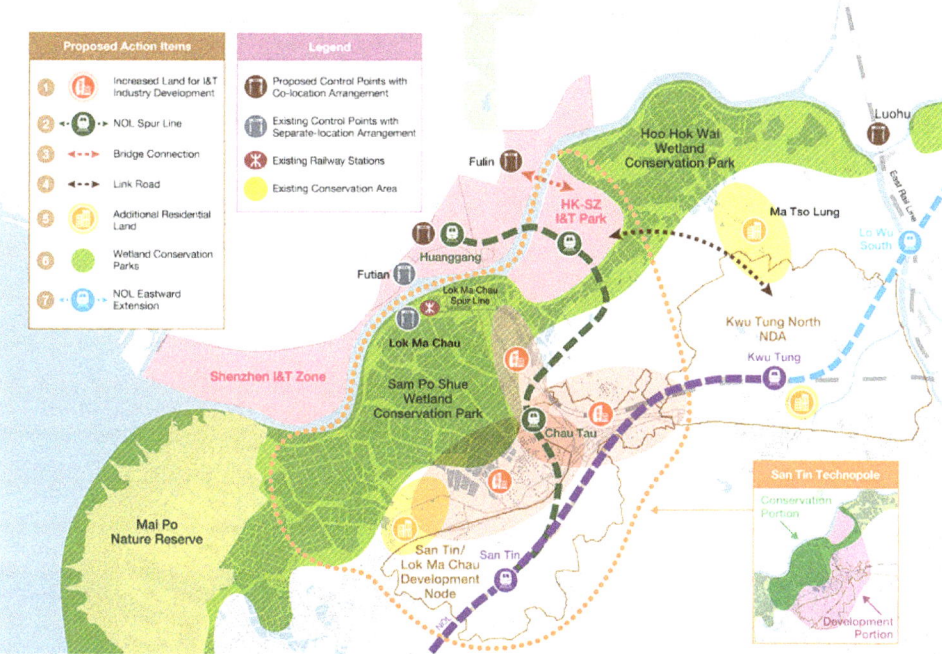

Figure 6.3: Wetland Conservation Parks. Reproduced by permission from the Development Bureau. ©2022 Development Bureau, Government of the Hong Kong Special Administrative Region of the People's Republic of China.

- The total area of these parks is about 1,220 hectares. It is estimated that private wetlands and fishponds to be resumed can amount to a total of 700 hectares, equivalent to 57% of the total, which the new, enhanced, ex-gratia compensation rates discussed below should facilitate.
- There will also be a need for a concomitant increase and enhancement of the capacity to properly manage these large areas of conservation parks, probably by a combination of both public sector and suitable NGOs, or along the lines of Mai Po Nature Reserve run by WWF-Hong Kong.

4) Large-Scale Housing Land Expansion Projects

- Expanding Hung Shui Kiu/Ha Tin NDA to areas in Lau Fau Shan and Tsim Bei Tsui.
- Examining development potential in areas from Lau Fau Shan to Pak Nai.
- Expanding Kwu Tung North NDA to Ma Tso Lung area.
- Developing Lo Wu and Man Kam To as a comprehensive development node.

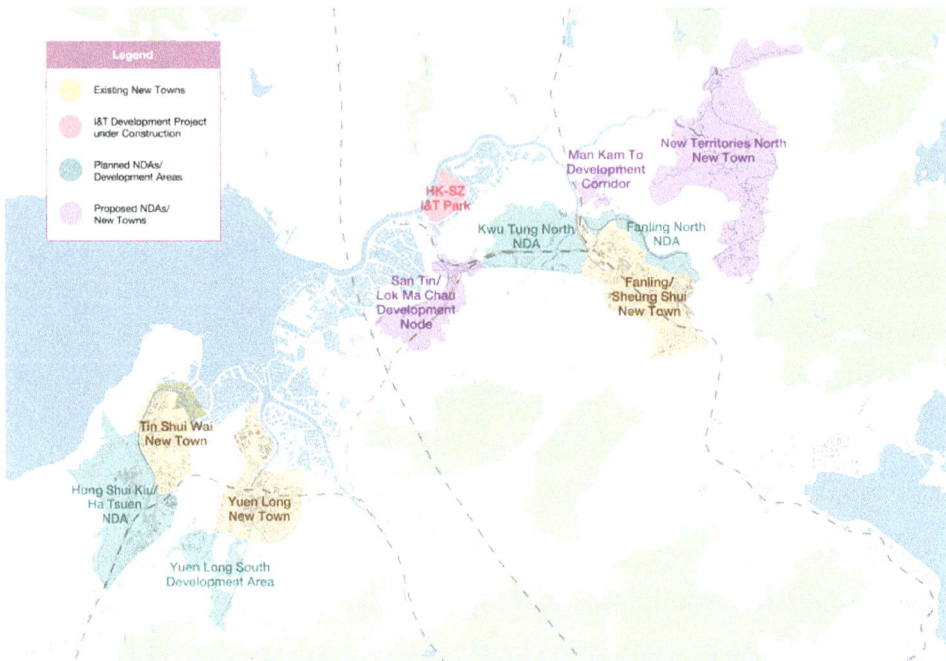

Figure 6.4: Large-scale housing land expansion projects. Reproduced by permission from the Development Bureau. ©2022 Development Bureau, Government of the Hong Kong Special Administrative Region of the People's Republic of China.

5) New Railway Projects

- Cross-boundary rail link between Hung Shui Kiu/Ha Tin NDA and Qianhai to provide a direct link to the Qianhai Shenzhen-Hong Kong Modern Service Industry Cooperation Zone. Established in 2010, the Zone now reports that there are about 11,500 Hong Kong-invested, innovation-driven enterprises that have provided close to HK$29.6 billion in capital, becoming increasingly significant in Qianhai's economy.
- Northward extension of NOL and connecting with the new Huanggang border crossing point via the Hong Kong-Shenzhen Innovation and Technology Park.
- Extension of East Rail Line to Louhu in Shenzhen and provision of Lo Wu South Station not for boundary crossing.
- Eastward extension of NOL from Kwu Tung Station, connecting Lo Wu, Man Kam To, Heung Yuen Wai, Ping Che, Ta Kwu Ling, and Queens Hill to Fanling with ten new stations.
- Examining Tsim Bei Tsui, Lau Fau Shan, and Pak Nai automated people mover.

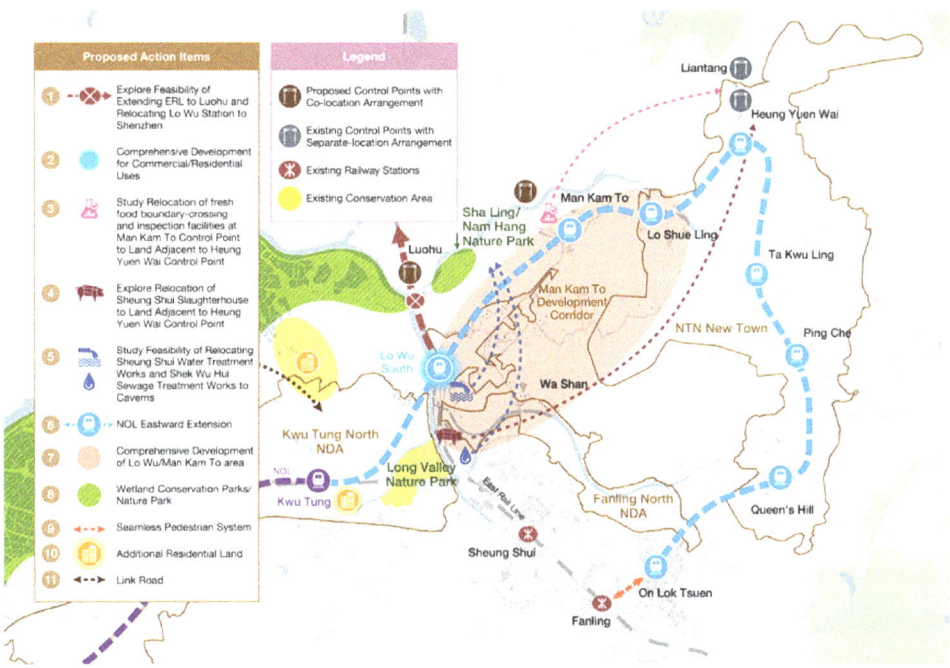

Figure 6.5: New Railway projects. Reproduced by permission from the Development Bureau. ©2022 Development Bureau, Government of the Hong Kong Special Administrative Region of the People's Republic of China.

Summary of Development Strategy

- Further develop about 600 hectares of housing and development land.
- Further provide about 165,000 to 186,000 residential units, equivalent to 13–14.5 Tai Koo Shings in number. A good start has been made with the first phase expansion of Kwu Tung North NDA, now underway, with the first 68 hectares of private land having been resumed in 2019. This will yield 21,000 residential units, 18,000 of which will be public housing for an additional population of 52,900, with the intake scheduled from 2023 to 2026.
- Further provide about 66,000 to 68,000 I&T jobs.
- Formation of a comprehensive system of wetlands and coastal ecological conservation of about 2,000 hectares.
- The target is to eventually accommodate a residential population of about 2.5 million and provide 650,000 jobs, including about 150,000 I&T jobs.

Hong Kong has never before attempted such a broad and ambitious plan, so it is crucial to have the necessary structures in place to deliver this outcome. One of the key action directions is to re-engineer the administrative mechanism and the operation processes. All of the previous major infrastructure projects such as the New Towns and the new airport were very much engineering-led. However, now that conservation and quality of life elements will be included in planning on an equal basis right from the start, very skilful and dedicated personnel will be required to integrate engineering elements and the right administrative structure in order to balance out leadership and deliver these occasionally competing requirements.

A common criticism of local governance is the 'separate silo' mentality that prevails between different bureaux, which can frustrate and delay implementation of new policies. A new structure will be needed to overcome the problem if this ambitious vision is to be delivered on time and within budget. In June 2023, the high powered Northern Metropolis Co-ordination Office was established as a cross-bureaux and cross-departmental entity whose action agenda for implementation of the development of the Northern Metropolis, which will span across 20 years, has the ambitious target to release all land use and development proposals before the end of 2024; commence land resumption on or before 2027 for 40% of new development land; and for 40% of the new flats to be completed by 2032 (as stated in paragraph 92 of the 2023 CE's Policy Address) (Lee 2023).

Subsequent Follow-Up Actions

1. The Financial Secretary (2024) in his 2024–25 budget announced a re-prioritization of capital works so that the site formation and infrastructure work for the Northern Metropolis can continue, whereas the Kau Yi Chau Artificial Islands is likely to be held back. These works will be funded by the issuance of government bonds of about HK$95 billion to HK$135 billion per annum. In effect, this means that the formulation of development plans for the four land formation projects under Action Items 1 and 4 above can now proceed at full speed. Also, the implementation of the NDA projects, including their expansion, can also be stepped up to ensure timely completion of housing projects. The Kwu Tung North NDA expansion discussed above is a good example, which will be helped by the timely introduction of the enhanced package of ex-gratia compensation discussed below.

2. On 3 May 2022, the Development Bureau (2022) announced, with immediate effect, a much-enhanced package of ex-gratia compensation that should significantly facilitate the land acquisition process. The plan now in place merges the original four locational zones into two user category zones, namely 'Tier One Zone' (applicable to land required for development uses such as NDAs, residential, economic development, and related public facilities) with the ex-gratia compensation rate for agricultural land re-set at the new Zone A rate of HK$1,510 per square foot (HK$16,254 per square metre) and 'Tier Two Zone' (applicable to land required for non-development purposes including rural

improvement and conservation uses) with the compensation rate set at half the Tier One rate, i.e. HK$755 per square foot (HK$8,127 per square metre). This latter figure will greatly assist the implementation of Action Item 3 above.

As before these rates will be reviewed half yearly.

Specific Planning and Implementation Points

1. It is recognized that the only way forward to deal with the multiple and complex land issues associated with New Territories land is for the government to undertake large scale land resumption and then clearance, which the new ex-gratia compensation rates will greatly facilitate. However, land resumption can only take place once a 'public purpose' has been established. The implementation of a statutory Outline Zoning Plan (OZP) has long been recognized as being such a 'public purpose'. This will now require the Planning Department to allocate the right level of resources so that the new OZPs can be completed and ready for implementation in a timely manner. The three rounds of public consultations that were undertaken prior to the Kwun Tung North NDA plan being approved (2013–2018) took some five years to complete, serving as a lesson learned. A more efficient and streamlined approach will be needed for the timely implementation of the NMDS, with probably just one round of consolidated consultations taking place.

2. Barely touched upon in the strategy is one of the big blights on the NT landscape, which are the many container storage areas which, with their necessary support vehicles, usually long and articulated, often operate on narrow and unsuitable roads – a perfect example of haphazard, unplanned land use that we now call brownfield sites. It must be remembered that these container storage areas came into being in the 1980s and 90s with the expansion of the container terminal; the government did not provide sufficient land for on-site container storage, resulting in the operators looking for alternative, cost effective, off-site options. Although the throughput at the Kwai Chung Container Terminals is lower than before, there will still be an ongoing need for land for container storage. This should be properly planned for in consultation with the container industry and in the right location together with the suitable road access; it should be included in the overall development strategy. Providing relocation sites will greatly facilitate and speed up land resumption and clearance. It should be anticipated that those container storage areas in existence on or before 1991 will be able to claim existing user rights and they will likely push not only for higher compensation but also for relocation as part of their compensation packages.

In 2021, Liber Research Community identified close to 2,000 hectares of brownfield sites compared with the government figure of 1,579 hectares. The discrepancy came about because the government had excluded older sites that were now revegetated.

The construction industry is another big user of brownfield land, with open storage of metal beams, cranes, boom lifts, and other equipment taking up some 115 hectares of such land.

In a written reply to a Legislative Council question on 7 December 2022, the Secretary for Development (2022) advised that around 1,000 hectares of these brownfield sites will gradually be developed for high-density housing and other uses related to the implementation of the new development plans.

On 14 April 2023, the Town Planning Board (TPB) approved revised TPB Planning Guideline No.13 F (PG13F) (2023) relating to applications for open storage and port back-up uses under s.16 of their ordinance. The TPB paper acknowledged that many existing brownfield operations have been or will be displaced as a result of government's intensified actions in implementing the NDAs and other projects related to the NMDS. Over the past few years, about 30 hectares of brownfield sites involving about 400 operators have been resumed and cleared. It is expected that the total brownfield area to be resumed and cleared from now up until 2026 will increase sharply to 200 hectares. There are four categories of site under PG13F and the revised guidelines significantly expand Category 2 areas from 281 to 602 hectares. Category 2 areas mostly lack clear planning intention or fixed development programmes; will be affected by major infrastructure projects; or are within or close to existing clusters of open storage/port back-up or other types of brownfield site with temporary uses.

The s.16 applications will require appropriate technical assessments for each site and, in particular, they should not be subject to high flooding risk. If there major adverse departmental comments or local objections can be resolved, temporary approvals of up to three years can be granted. The cost and time of making such submissions and the relatively short term of approval may prove to be a deterrent to those displaced operators who need to relocate elsewhere. Legitimate concerns have been raised by various environmental groups that this initiative could become counter-productive as they would likely, in turn, result in the creation of additional future brownfield sites.

For many of these types of user that cannot be relocated into multi-storey buildings but have otherwise made recognizable contributions to the local economy, more thought now needs to be given to providing some suitable, longer-term relocation sites so they can continue to operate and be willing to move.

For those who can operate in multi-storey buildings, the outlook seems a bit brighter. The government has reserved five sites totalling 72 hectares of land with a potential gross floor area of 3.9 million square metres in Hung Shui Kiu, Ha Tsuen, NDA, and Yuen Long South Development Area for multi-storey building development. This can be used to accommodate affected brownfield operators who are able to relocate to such buildings. It is hoped that these buildings will be in place from 2027 to 2028 and at least

30% of the floor space taken up by the government for leasing to displaced brownfield operators at a rental comparable to prevailing market rentals of the brownfield sites.

3. Through working together with the Shenzhen authorities, a magnificent opportunity emerged to create a north-south ecological corridor over Wutong Mountain, Robin's Nest, and Pat Sin Leng, which would be necessary to conserve and enhance the overall natural landscape, ecology, and habitat resources. In May 2019, environmental NGOs produced the Robin's Nest Joint Statement and Plan that covered 1,120 hectares – 95% of which is government land – and recommended the most suitable boundary for the Robin's Nest Country Park.

It was most disappointing therefore when, in March 2024, the government announced the establishment of Robin's Nest Country Park but bowed to pressure from the local villagers to exclude their burial grounds, which then resulted in an area of only about 530 hectares. This small size is clearly unfit for the purpose, particularly as the proposed southern boundaries are not contiguous with Pat Sin Leng Country Park and defeats the whole purpose of this ecological corridor. It runs contrary to the second planning principle of the NMDS, 'Proactive conservation'! As demonstrated elsewhere, NT burial grounds and country parks are not mutually exclusive and can co-exist together.

Figure 6.6: Wutong Mountain/Robin's Nest/Pat Sin Leng, North-South Ecological Corridor. Reproduced by permission from the Development Bureau ©2022 Development Bureau, Government of the Hong Kong Special Administrative Region of the People's Republic of China.

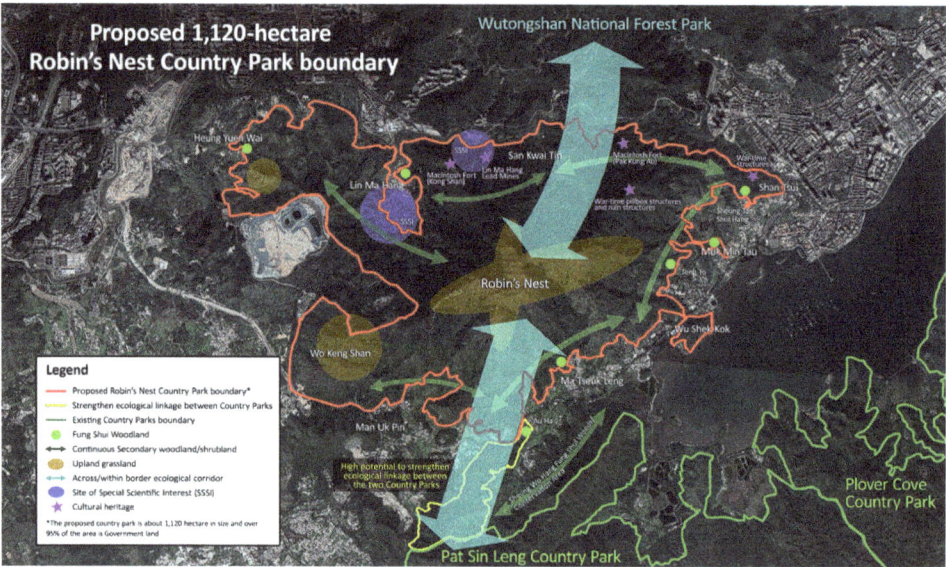

Figure 6.7: Proposed 1120-hectare Robin's Nest Country Park boundary. Illustration courtesy of Suet Mei Wong, Hong Kong Bird Watching Society.

The NGOs continue to lobby for the larger area to eventually be gazetted, so the opportunity for Hong Kong to properly contribute to the development of this ecological corridor is not lost. The 2019 plan would ensure a much wider area under improved management, particularly for protection from hill fires under the Country Park Regulations, as well as enhanced conservation that will significantly increase the carrying capacity of this ecological corridor.

4. Following the articulation of Planning Principles 1, 2 and in particular 3, the retention of Fanling Golf Course in its entirety is well justified so that it can continue providing a readymade location for eco-recreation and education whilst at the same time preserving extremely rare habitats, including that of the critically endangered Chinese swamp cypress. With its luxuriant green open spaces incorporating mature woodlands, it already has a long history of recreational and high landscape value as it provides these functions today in a well-regulated manner that benefits the community both locally and internationally. Given its prime location, and properly curated as at present, there is no reason why it should not become the high quality, green lung Central Park the new metropolis deserves with golf and public enjoyment coexisting.

This point of view was endorsed in December 2023 when Fanling Golf Course was given an Award of Distinction in the 2023 UNESCO Asia-Pacific Heritage Awards for Cultural Heritage Conservation programmes. The concluding sentence in their citation reads 'The Fanling Golf Course project thus represents a major advancement in the promotion of an inclusive conservation management for cultural landscapes in both Hong Kong and the larger region.'

5. Care needs to be taken with regard to both the location and type of activity envisaged in any new outdoor eco-recreational facility that may be proposed. Inappropriate use and excess human traffic could have huge negative impact on the local habitats and environment. For example, birds are well known to be hypersensitive to human activity – hence the need for hides and controlled numbers visiting Mai Po. By comparison, the restoration of agricultural activity at the Lai Chi Wo project is proving to be extremely popular; nevertheless, there will soon be a need to control traffic so as not to overload the sewage and drainage systems, which could result in polluting overflows into the adjacent Yan Chau Tong Marine Park. This delicate balance needs to properly be understood before proceeding with any new facilities.

6. The four new railway projects with ten new stations outlined in Action Item 5 above will provide a solid transport framework and backbone to the Twin Cities, something that should positively encourage the private sector to fully participate in the development of the new metropolis. Landowners and developers should examine both their existing land holdings and land banks as well as future land sales, particularly those that will be close to future stations, to review what would be the highest and best use of those sites given their enhanced connectivity. Timely applications for planning approvals and lease modifications should be put in place. For example, the existing On Lok Tsuen Industrial Area in Fanling, where 2.5 plot ratio industrial use has previously been permitted, will be rezoned as 'Other Use-Business & IT' which would be a good incentive for a review both for change of use as well as development intensity.

7. If the Technopole is to truly become Hong Kong's Silicon Valley, there will be a strong need for significant private sector participation to create the right balance and types of community associated with this vision. In order to get non-government agencies involved, quite a lot – perhaps up to 50% – of the newly created land will need to be disposed of by way of public tender. However, there will be a strong case to restrict the lease conditions user clause for these sites to I&T, research, development and design, and similar related activities to ensure that the right mix of end users can be achieved. Consideration should also be given to allowing some residential accommodation so that workers in these industries can have the convenience, if they so wish, of being located on site.

8. Colliers, a leading diversified real estate and professional services and investment management company, issued a thought-provoking paper in May 2022 entitled 'Northern Metropolis: A Vision for All' in which they introduce the idea of high-quality living for seniors that in a properly planned and developed environment could offer reliable yields for investors (Colliers 2022). This was followed in May 2023 by JLL Hong Kong (Han et al. 2023) whose report 'The Rise of Senior Living' advised that the underlying

statistics of Hong Kong's rapidly ageing population are compelling, with the number of people aged 65 and over likely to nearly double from 1.32 million (18.4%) of the total population in 2019 to 2.52 million (33.3%) in 2039. These figures are supported by the recent projections of the Census and Statistics Department in their Hong Kong Projections 2022–2046 (2023), with 1.45 million or 20% of the total population now aged 65 or over and increasing to 2.74 million or 36% in 2046.

The current private sector provision is a mere 1,500 living spaces for elderly, scattered around Hong Kong without extra facilities such as swimming pools, gym, hobby rooms, or opportunities to engage with a regular community. There would appear to be a huge gap in provision, which should attract some private sector interest, particularly as an increasing number of affluent elderly residents will want to live independently and have active lifestyles in their twilight years.

A possible financial model that could be considered for such projects could be along the lines of a Real Estate Investment Trust (REITs), which Hong Kong is now familiar with. Developers, operators, and other private equity funds should collaborate to form a REIT that provides long-term, low-cost financing for the development and operation of the project. Each stakeholder would have a distinct role in the project allowing even distribution of profit and risk among the joint venture partners. Such a development should be able to fit in well with the visionary planning that has taken place so far. If the developers involved do not have a suitable site in their land bank, the government could potentially make a suitable site (or multiple sites) available by way of tender within one of the NDAs to enable private sector development, possibly on a public–private partnership model. This could help unlock this sector and diversify the population balance in the Northern Metropolis. It is encouraging to note that the CE's 2023 Policy Address acknowledges the need to leverage market forces to expedite development (Lee 2023).

Northern Metropolis Action Agenda

This action agenda (Hong Kong SAR Government 2023) was unveiled in November 2023 and outlines the development positioning of the four major zones in the Northern Metropolis: the High-end Professional Services and Logistics Hub; the I&T Zone; the Boundary Commerce and Industry Zone; and the Blue and Green Recreation, Tourism and Conservation Circle. Their development represents an evolution of the 'Twin Cities, Three Circles' concept introduced in the NMDS.

Regrettably, the Northern Metropolis Action Agenda remains silent on two important NMDS action items; Item 29, the Urban Rural Greenway Policy going east to west across the Northern Metropolis and Item 19, the Comprehensive Ecological Habitat Network Policy. These omissions are troubling because it seems that there has been little or no attempt to comply with the first two planning principles of striking a balance between 'urban-rural integration' and 'proactive conservation', with development proposals now appearing to be taking precedence over conservation objectives.

On the same theme, there are growing concerns regarding the proposals for the Sam Po Shui Wetland Conservation Park described above, which has a quoted area of 520 hectares. This same Wetland Conservation Park is discussed in paragraph 154(ii) of the 2023 Policy Address (Lee 2023), which talks about establishing this park to enhance ecological quality and biodiversity of the Northern Metropolis and providing quality outdoor eco-education and recreational facilities for public enjoyment.

However, it has now been revealed that the principal function of this Wetland Conservation Park, which has on closer examination shrunk to 338 hectares, will be to offset the loss of ecological and fisheries as a result of filling in of some 89 hectares of fishponds and wetlands as reclamation to provide a total of 300 hectares of I&T land for the San Tin Technopole. It is therefore apparent that government's actions contradict their own planning principles, resulting in damage to the existing fragile ecosystem that requires parallel compensatory measures and will struggle to enhance environmental capacity in this location. Again, the suspicion is that 'development' is taking precedence over 'conservation' with the government failing to find the right balance.

This suspicion was confirmed by Lands Department's Gazette Notification No. GN 1322, dated 8 March 2024, which announced the statutory land resumption of 1,776 private lots with an area of about 171 hectares for the implementation of San Tin Technopole (Phase 1) but with no suggestion of acquiring any of the land required for the implementation of the Sham Po Shue Wetland Conservation Park.

Shenzhen is now firmly established as the undisputed Chinese information and technology equivalent of the United States' Silicon Valley, with heavyweights such as Huawei, Tencent, BYD, and DJI already established and operating there and, moreover, acting as a magnet for new companies to join them. It was reported that some 86 start-up companies were planned there for 2024 (Failory 2024). By comparison, the local Office for Attracting Strategic Enterprises announced on 20 March 2024 that twenty-four strategic enterprises, including nineteen from the first batch and six from the second batch, have agreed to come here. These figures alone give a clear indication of how difficult it will be for Hong Kong to establish a foothold in this market.

So, given the twin challenges of competition with Shenzhen and the potential for huge environmental damage in the sensitive area immediately adjacent to the Mai Po Nature Reserve, there seems to be a good case for adopting a precautionary approach by proceeding in phases. This will not only help assess the true, cumulative environmental impacts but also, just as importantly, properly test the marketability of all this newly created I&T land.

A suitable first phase would be to stay focused on the development of the Lok Ma Chau Loop that covers an area of 87.7 hectares, of which 53.49 hectares have been earmarked for research and development, education, and culture and creative industries. At the same time, the newly recommended measures to enhance the ecological and biodiversity of Sham Po Shue Wetland Conservation Park should be started so that their true effectiveness can be assessed before further reclamations are undertaken in this location.

It is evident from the above comments and observations that there is an urgent need to effectively monitor these potentially conflicting activities and ensure the principles of the NMDS do not become compromised. This important role clearly falls within the terms of reference of the Development Subcommittee and Environmental Affairs Subcommittee of the Legislative Council, both of whom need to take action immediately. The professional institutions of the architects, planners, and surveyors, together with the various Chambers of Commerce and the Urban Land Institute, should also have a role to play in keeping an eye on the government's performance and actions.

The quality-of-life conservation policies of the NMDS are fully justified as the most cost-effective way of investing public funds to provide a balanced lifestyle for the future population of the Northern Metropolis. They will be able to enjoy the benefits of being resident in a liveable city with a good quality of life and with due respect for heritage and nature conservation. This will also help our integration with the Greater Bay Area by promoting our regional, national, and international obligations which, in turn, will all help to re-establish Hong Kong as a global city.

References

Census and Statistics Department. 2023. *Hong Kong Population Projections 2022–2046*. https://www.censtatd.gov.hk/en/data/stat_report/product/B1120015/att/B1120015092023XXXXB01.pdf.

Chan, Wendy, Kathryn Han, Tom Parker, and Olivia Ng. 2023. 'The Rise of Senior Living'. JLL Hong Kong. https://www.jll.com.hk/en/trends-and-insights/research/the-rise-of-senior-living.

Colliers. 2022. *Northern Metropolis: A Vision for All*. https://www.colliers.com/download-article?itemId=c4534325-3fc9-43ee-b197-a939f2a70e23.

Development Bureau. 2022. 'Enhancements to the compensation arrangements for landowners and business operators affected by land resumption and clearance projects of the Government.' https://www.devb.gov.hk/en/publications_and_press_releases/press/index_id_11194.html

Failory. 2024. 'Top 86 Startups in Shenzhen in 2024'. Last modified 9 February, 2024. www.failory.com/startups/shenzhen.

Financial Secretary, Hong Kong SAR Government. 2024. 'The 2024–25 Budget'. https://www.budget.gov.hk/2024/eng/estimates.html

Hong Kong Special Administrative Region of the People's Republic of China. 2023. *Northern Metropolis Action Agenda*. https://www.nm.gov.hk/downloads/NM_Eng_Booklet_Web.pdf.

Lee, John. 2021. *Northern Metropolis Development Strategy*. Policy Address. https://www.policyaddress.gov.hk/2021/eng/pdf/publications/Northern/Northern-Metropolis-Development-Strategy-Report.pdf.

Lee, John. 2022. *The Chief Executive's 2022 Policy Address*. Policy Address. https://www.policyaddress.gov.hk/2022/en/policy.html.

Lee, John. 2023. *The Chief Executive's 2023 Policy Address*. Policy Address. https://www.policyaddress.gov.hk/2023/en/policy.html.

Planning Department. 2016. *Hong Kong 2030+: Towards a Planning and Vision and Strategy Transcending 2030*. Archived 19 February, 2023 at https://web.archive.org/web/20230219111620/https://www.pland.gov.hk/pland_en/p_study/comp_s/hk2030plus/document/2030+Booklet_Eng.pdf.

Secretary for Development, Hong Kong SAR Government. 2022. 'LegCo Question LCQ2'. Press Releases. https://www.devb.gov.hk/en/publications_and_press_releases/press/index_id_11378.html.

Town Planning Board. 2023. 'Town Planning Board Guidelines for Application for Open Storage and Port Back-Up Uses Under Section 16 of The Town Planning Ordinance.' Town Planning Board, TPG PG-No. 13F. https://www.tpb.gov.hk/en/forms/Guidelines/pg13f_e.pdf.

Northern Metropolis Development Strategy: Commentary (NC)

The NMDS is the hugely ambitious and far-reaching urbanisation plan announced by the HKSAR Government in 2021 to address long-standing needs for housing as well as growing connections with the Greater Bay Area of Southern China. The scope of future development encompasses the Yuen Long and Northern Districts of Hong Kong, spanning a total land area of about 30,000 hectares with an overall strategy that the government has encapsulated with the slogan of 'Twin Cities, Three Circles'.

The NMDS offers a more pragmatic development alternative to the previously announced Lantau Tomorrow Vision, also known as the Kau Yi Chau Artificial Islands, a massive land reclamation project of 1,700 hectares in the eastern waters of Lantau Island. When first introduced by the HKSAR Government in 2018, Lantau Tomorrow Vision was immediately met with wide public criticism both for its tremendous cost (one-half of the government's total fiscal reserves) as well as adverse environmental impact, as this development plan would require over 260 million cubic metres of filling material (Ng 2018).

Historically, Hong Kong has never had a land shortage problem – only a land management problem. Most notably, in the New Territories, there are close to 2,000 hectares of brownfield sites, many of which have potential for development of housing (Greenpeace 2021).

As noted above by Nissim in his 'Specific Planning and Implementation Points', brownfield sites represent 'haphazard and unplanned land use' largely occupied by container storage areas. Surely there must be 32 hectares of brownfield site immediately available for housing development in lieu of the same land area to be resumed by the government from the historic Hong Kong Golf Club, which would be a stark contradiction of two of the NMDS core planning principles of environmental conservation and more eco-recreation facilities (Hung 2023).

The NMDS aims to build 165,000–186,000 new residential units over 600 hectares of land development which will house part of a total population of 2.5 million residents in the northern New Territories. If conservation and other issues are truly taken into consideration, what will be the ensuing model for future development besides the usual 30-storey towers atop podiums interspersed with 3-storey New Territories exempt village houses?

Alternatively, is there another building typology that still achieves overall requirements of sufficient density while also giving emphasis to neighbourhoods with walkable environments and mixed-use facilities to accommodate an increasingly ageing demographic? One with greater promotion and protection of biodiversity that still integrates natural greenery and gardens in public housing as in several notable examples, both built and planned, in Singapore (CNN 2021)?

Thus, on its own merits, the NMDS needs to demonstrate that it will be more than simply an engineering-led infrastructure development and that it can truly fulfil its own stated planning principles, including: urban-rural integration, environmental conservation, and eco-recreation and tourism facilities. And it needs to show that its built outcome will hopefully result in bona fide placemaking, not simply policy and marketing slogans, that fulfil the original definition of 'city' – from the Latin word *civitas* – meaning a 'community of citizens' with the shared pursuit of a better life in a more liveable condition.

Figure 6.8: The fish ponds at Hoo Hok Wai, a patch of wetland next to the Lok Ma Chau Loop, which is part of the Wetland Improvement Area at The Northern Metropolis Development Strategy. Photograph courtesy of *South China Morning Post.*

Key Notes

1. Not a land shortage problem, but a land management problem.
2. Building typology for housing other than 30-storey towers.
3. Planning principles for Northern Metropolis Development Strategy.

References

Greenpeace. 2021. *Missing Brownfields – Hong Kong Brownfields Report 2021.* https://issuu.com/greenpeace_eastasia/docs/missing_brownfields_-_hong_kong_brownfields_report.

Holland, Oscar. 2021. 'Singapore Is Building a 42,000-Home Eco "Smart" City.' *CNN*, 1 February. https://edition.cnn.com/style/article/singapore-tengah-eco-town/index.html.

Hung, Emily. 2023. 'Hong Kong Golf Association Warns Building Public Housing on Part of City's Oldest Course Will "Suffocate" Future of Sport.' *South China Morning Post*, 12 May. https://www.scmp.com/news/hong-kong/health-environment/article/3220294/hong-kong-golf-association-warns-building-public-housing-part-citys-oldest-course-will-suffocate.

Ng, Naomi. 2018. 'Hong Kong "Throwing Money into Sea" with Proposed Reclamation Project for New Town, Concern Groups Warn.' *South China Morning Post*, 11 October. https://www.scmp.com/news/hong-kong/society/article/2168185/hong-kong-throwing-money-sea-proposed-reclamation-project-new.

Afterword: From Space to Place and Humane Urbanism

Nelson Chen

One of my first college classes in architecture, still memorable from over five decades ago, centred on a spirited discussion about 'What is architecture?' with comparisons of several definitions of architecture from the most fundamental and technical ('the art and technique of designing and building') to the artistic and lyrical ('the learned game, correct and magnificent, of forms assembled in the light', according to visionary modernist architect Le Corbusier).

Towards the end of this discussion and debate, my Harvard professor, Albert Szabo, shared his own personal definition of architecture as 'the design of spaces for human activity'. Moreover, he added, 'good architecture supports and enables those activities; great architecture *inspires* them'.

This understanding is reinforced with profound insight about architecture and its impact – unexpectedly not from a famous architect but from Winston Churchill, who observed, 'We shape our buildings; thereafter, they shape us.' Expanded to a larger urban scale, the same might be observed for placemaking in our neighbourhoods and cities – how do they ultimately shape us as a society? In the design of space, how and when does abstract space become occupied place, whether at the scale of buildings, neighbourhoods, or cities? To support, enable, and, hopefully, even inspire our human activities?

Unlike individual buildings that reflect the architect's vision, urban form represents a more collective will within a culture unique to that community. This has been the consistent theme and design methodology of a Pritzker Prize-winning architect, the late Fumihiko Maki, throughout his acclaimed career. As a young academic in the US, Maki authored an influential treatise titled 'Investigations in Collective Form' first published in 1964. It was required reading for architecture students of my generation in the 1970s. Perhaps in

Figure 7.1a: Hillside Terrace in Tokyo. Photograph courtesy of a+t architecture publishers.

Figure 7.1b: Hillside Terrace in Tokyo. Photograph courtesy of a+t architecture publishers.

reaction to the prevailing interest in those years of megastructures such as the Tokyo Project and others, this critical study by Maki focused instead on the city as formed by open spaces rather than building masses, respecting the specific character of an urban site, and the knitting together of buildings, urban spaces, streets, and footpaths (Maki 2018).

As he described it, 'Collective Form' represented groups of buildings – not single structures unrelated to each other – that have reason to be together over time and the resulting city as a pattern of events. At Hillside Terrace in Tokyo, this vision was realized as a kind of urban design lab that the practice of Maki and Associates designed incrementally over twenty-three years in six successive stages.

Its lesson and legacy are for us to remember that while architecture may ultimately be art, it is always a social art in service of society. Our ultimate goal should not be designing iconic buildings as objects but creating iconic places for people and their activities.

Thus, it is essential for all stakeholders – academic, professional, and especially the public at large – to understand their city as an urban lab that co-creates new knowledge and understanding of what constitutes truly sustainable development. In Hong Kong and throughout Asia, that sustainable development encompasses both high-density, high-rise urbanisation on the one hand and preserving what remains of the natural environment on the other.

From the case studies presented in this volume, placemaking operates at multiple scales – from gardens and parks in dense urban neighbourhoods to placekeeping in rural villages such as Lai Chi Wo; from elevated footbridges in Central to pedestrianised networks such as Taikoo Place; from mega-form urban complexes such as ICC and Taikoo Place to the formation of New Towns in the New Territories and the planned Northern Metropolis Development Strategy.

In this regard, the definition and understanding of placemaking is now being expanded by Roger Nissim beyond the original notions introduced by Jane Jacobs and William Whyte in order to encompass a much larger scale of urban and regional development with distinctive identity and characteristics defined by site context and morphology as well as the appropriate balance of built density, open space, mixed uses, linkage, and walkability. This definition also includes the notion and necessity of placekeeping to sustain the initial success of placemaking.

The origins of placemaking in North America in the 1970s were largely motivated by revitalising the downtowns of cities abandoned in favour of suburban living and mega mall shopping centres sustained by a lifestyle dependent on ubiquitous roads and cars. Land policy researchers such as Mark Wyckoff addressed various strategies to attract people back to the city by providing quality places – both public and private – to attract population, jobs, and income growth as well as achieve economic development benefits (Wyckoff et al. 2015).

From their historic origins, the oldest cities were experienced and understood from a human perspective while walking, say, five kilometres per hour. In the modern metropolis, new cities are largely experienced from motor vehicles at sixty kilometres per hour. As noted

Afterword 107

Figure 7.2: LA Spaghetti Junction. Photograph courtesy of Kevin Payravi on Wikimedia Commons.

by the renowned urbanist Jan Gehl, the two predominant paradigms of twentieth century urban planning were 'modernism and motorism', leading to larger and larger buildings as *objects* with leftover spaces in between and not people-friendly cities filled with human-scaled *places*. According to Gehl, modern cities must transition back from a 'traffic place' to a 'people place'.

As noted previously in this volume, Hong Kong residents enjoy less than 2.8 square metres of open space per person in its built-over land area, which is about one-half of Tokyo (5.8 square metres) and roughly one-third of Singapore (7.4 square metres) or Shanghai (7.8 square metres) – in any case, significantly below the World Health Organization (WHO) recommended standards of 9 square metres per person (Lai 2017). In the context of this high-density, high-rise urban condition, the few opportunities to capture physical space for placemaking then become paramount – whether indoors or outdoors, above ground or below, permanent or pop-up. Without these pockets of accessible social space for people and human activities, the stated goals of developing an equitable, healthy, and sustainable city are reduced to empty slogans rather than effective urban strategies.

More often than not, however, these urban pocket spaces may be found interspersed among residential developments or adjacent to traffic roads with a high ratio of hardscape vs soft landscaping, reflecting an 'engineering approach' that favours low maintenance over a more 'nature-based solution' with more trees and planting to offer basic human comfort from shading and vegetation to mitigate urban heat island effects and stormwater stagnation (Thilakaratne 2019).

It says something about the paucity of placemaking in densely developed Hong Kong that one of the most popular public spaces in the city in recent years has been the Western District Cargo Working Area – commonly known as 'Instagram Pier' – with its spectacular harbour views, especially at sunset. Even though it is not technically a public space, 'Instagram Pier' was popularly recognized in the 2013 Hong Kong Public Space Awards co-organised by Designing Hong Kong and Hong Kong Public Space Initiative. Despite its widespread popularity, the pier was closed in 2020 without prior notice by the government with a warning of HK$10,000 in fines and six months in prison for members of the public caught entering this restricted working area.

Figure 7.3a: Western District Pier. Photograph courtesy of Nelson Chen.

Figure 7.3b: Western District Pier. Photograph courtesy of Nelson Chen.

Figure 7.4: Looking down the escalator system on Shelley Street, from above Elgin Street. Photograph courtesy of yeowatzup on Wikimedia Commons.

Another unique and popular example of Hong Kong placemaking is the Mid-Levels to Central escalator, a covered pedestrian walkway that is the world's longest at 800 metres in length with 135 metres in climb that expands the definition and understanding of urban placemaking in the vertical dimension of a volumetric city characterised by high-rise density and connectivity.

And while it has been several decades in the making, the waterfront promenades on both Hong Kong and Kowloon sides of Victoria Harbour are finally taking shape as attractive and welcoming destinations for public enjoyment.

Despite extreme urban density, cramped living conditions and increasing income inequality as measured by the Gini Index, remarkable average life expectancy statistics from both the United Nations Development Programme and the World Bank reveal that Hong Kong ranks first in the world at 85.1 years (88.1 for women, 82.8 for men) (UNDP, 2023). These impressive statistics were maintained even in the aftermath of the recent COVID-19 pandemic and appear to reflect numerous factors including its public healthcare system, nutritional diet, low infant mortality, and others. One major contributor must be the 'enabling environment' of a safe, walkable, compact city with easy access to a highly efficient public transportation system that promotes a more physically active lifestyle.

If more strategically located and well-designed public places for human activities are added and integrated in the city, not only life expectancy but the quality of life itself shall be greatly increased for people of all ages. In so doing, these public spaces will better reflect the values and aspirations of our city at a collective scale toward achieving an ecological and humane urbanism.

References

Lai, Carine. 2017. *Unopened Space: Mapping Equitable Availability of Open Space in Hong Kong*. Civic Exchange, Hong Kong. https://civic-exchange.org/report/unopened-space-mapping-equitable-availability-of-open-space-in-hong-kong/.

Maki, Fumihiko, Yukitoshi Wakatsuki, Hidetoshi Ohno, Tokihiko Takatani, and Naomi R. Pollock. 2018. *City with a Hidden Past*. Translated by Hiroshi Watanabe. Kajima Institute Publishing Co., Ltd.

Thilakaratne, R. 2019. *Designing Liveable Open Urban Spaces in High Density Cities*. IOP Conference Series: Earth and Environmental Science. https://iopscience.iop.org/article/10.1088/1755-1315/297/1/012049.

United Nations Development Programme (UNDP). 2024. *Hong Kong, China (SAR)*. Human Development Reports. 8 September. http://hdr.undp.org/en/countries/profiles/HKG.

Wyckoff, Mark, Brad Neumann, Glenn Pape, and Kurt Schindler. 2015. *Economic Development Tool: A Placemaking Guidebook*. Michigan State University Land Policy Institute.

www.ingramcontent.com/pod-product-compliance
Ingram Content Group UK Ltd.
Pitfield, Milton Keynes, MK11 3LW, UK
UKHW060844160426
5217IPUK00043B/2101